Nathaniel Popkin is a ... that cut deep through th... license cruelty, revealing the brittle bones of an unjust, death-dealing culture. Everyone should read this book. It is clarifying, bracing, and ultimately transformative; truth-telling is essential for change, and change is essential.

—Kathleen Dean Moore,
author of *Great Tide Rising*

How can we go diligently about our business while the daily disasters of climate change are already visibly recasting natural processes, forcing migration and violence? "We are the most slippery kind of criminal," explains Nathaniel Popkin in his searching new book *To Reach the Spring*. And he's right, Americans (especially middle class and wealthy white Americans) have built up a resistance to the consciousness of their own complicity in the climate crisis. Exerting privilege without feeling privileged, we go about our quotidian consumption, and destruction, consumed by worry but never taking real action. Simultaneously told as a letter to a future descendant, a history of disaster, a personal confession, and a lie-stabbing op-ed, Popkin has crafted a read so melancholy and spiritual you won't lay it aside until you're done.

—Scott Gabriel Knowles,
author of *The Disaster Experts:
Mastering Risk in Modern America*

Also by Nathaniel Popkin

to
reach
the
spring

*From Complicity to Consciousness
in the Age of Eco-Crisis*

NATHANIEL POPKIN

NEW DOOR BOOKS
Philadelphia 2020

NEW DOOR BOOKS
An imprint of P. M. Gordon Associates, Inc.
2115 Wallace Street
Philadelphia, Pennsylvania 19130
U.S.A.

Cover design: Isaak Popkin

Cover photograph: Valley of the Possible in southern Chile,
photo by the author

Library of Congress Control Number: 2020940887
ISBN 978-0-9995501-6-8 (paperback)
ISBN 978-0-9995501-7-5 (e-book)

*Today, here, our only purpose
is to reach the spring.*

Primo Levi, *If This Is a Man*

In memory of my godfather,
David K. Kanter,
enchanted by the earth in all
its humble beauty

contents

to
reach
the
spring

preface

The pronouncements, all from Republican officials, came in the fourth week of March 2020. On television, Texas Lieutenant Governor Dan Patrick declared that elderly people, most vulnerable to disease caused by the novel coronavirus, COVID-19, would be willing to sacrifice their own lives in order to allow businesses, closed under stay-at-home orders, to reopen. Patrick was echoing the desire of the president of the United States, whose chief economic advisor, Larry Kudlow, had said, also on television, "The cure can't be worse than the disease, and we're gonna have to make some difficult tradeoffs." The tradeoffs he had in mind were the deaths of many thousands of people in exchange for a return to normal economic activity.

Many close observers of American politics saw these statements as evidence of panic on the part of the Republican party, worried over the reelection prospects of the president, Donald J. Trump. Mounting evidence revealed that Trump had badly bungled the response to the virus. His unwillingness to act despite knowledge of the severity of the disease and his mendacity, incompetence, and divisive rhetoric had turned the pandemic into an American tragedy: lives wrecked by death, illness, unemployment, and poverty, with no end in sight. Kudlow, Patrick, and other Republican officials floating the idea of "trade-off" were admitting that the president could not be reelected with a totally shattered economy; since he had failed to stop the spread of the disease, reopening business at any cost was the only chance.

But most Americans simply reacted in horror. There is no tradeoff when it comes to human life and no value to be put on it. No American—no human being—should be sacrificed so that businesses can go back to making profit.[1]

The righteous position, however, exposes an underlying truth about human life on planet Earth at the start of the third decade of the twenty-first century: the global capitalist economic system operates by virtue of this very tradeoff, of lives for profit. The only difference is that for a wealthy nation like the United States a high proportion of those lives are sacrificed at a far distance—in sweatshops, factories, rigs, mines, hothouses, and trawlers—and out of sight. As global capitalism demands cheap and disposable labor, it also

1. The Trump administration repeatedly has placed corporate profit and the value of the stock market above other economic goals, including job stability, equity in pay, and access to health care; the framing of the choice is theirs.

consumes living plants and animals—and the forests, oceans, and river systems where they live—not to mention the ore, minerals, crude oil, and metals dug out from below. All this we sacrifice without second thought. So tangled as we are in the intricacies of this system of sacrifice and profit—as workers, investors, consumers, victims—we can't seem to envision another way. The immense scale, and far reach, of the global economy overwhelms even the basic moral question: What is life worth?

At its most distilled, this is the question we must ask during a time of extreme environmental crisis, as man-made global warming, intensive pesticide and herbicide use, damming of rivers, incineration of forests, burning of fossil fuels, and the expansion of grazing land for meat production knocks ecological systems out of balance, with spiraling repercussions for species diversity and human health. What is life worth?

And how can the value we assign to it—assuming a stable and reliable "we" might emerge from the present state of competition and conflict—come to shape the human response to the ecological crisis—or for that matter, an immediate humanitarian crisis like COVID-19?

The coronavirus pandemic indeed has exposed, with the precision of an X-ray, the inadequacies, injustices, and vulnerabilities of American society. Extending the metaphor, the May 2020 police murder of George Floyd has, like an MRI, exposed the danger of the criminal justice system, which brutalizes African American men especially, exposing them to violence, over-crowded holding cells, and police without the training or the judgment to guard against the spread of the disease. This is on top of over-incarceration, at rates that far surpass other nations, which has created lethal hotspots inside our jails. For many years now, racial segregation and systemic racism have condemned millions of Americans to living in communities that lack adequate health care. Thirty million Americans have no health insurance, and without a national health care system the government response to the pandemic has been disjointed, inequitable, and fragmented. Reliance on contract workers leaves millions without employment stability. And COVID-19 seems to most easily kill the most unhealthy, those who are condemned by poverty and racism to live nearest to sources of lethal chemicals, such as refineries, farms using herbicides and pesticides, and factories. Many are also victims of the poor American diet based itself on the environmental catastrophe of cheap sugar cane, palm oil, corn, and beef, as well as polluted air and contaminated water.

Magnify these vulnerabilities to a global scale and, like the question of sacrifice and tradeoff, a terrifying picture is revealed, of billions of impoverished people, citizens of nations without even basic health care resources or environmental safeguards, left more or less helpless, in harm's way.

Pandemic, then, is a kind of dry run for eco-crisis, in its capacity to force us to compose questions, but also in teaching us where to seek answers. Whom do we trust enough to put aside questions of private interest in favor of the greater good? The overwhelming answer to this question is not elected officials,[2] but rather medical professionals, public health experts, and scientists—those on the ground and in labs, those modeling and interpreting data, those able to observe how even disparate inputs interact in dynamic entanglements.

But after a half-century or more of intensifying scientific research on climate change and the vivid interpretation of mounting data that prove the extent and the danger of damaged ecological systems, we have mostly ignored the warnings of scientists. Casting aside their elaborate models, we have instead allowed the market, and political figures dedicated to protecting it, to determine the future of life on the planet. The global experience with COVID-19 begs for a reconsideration. The market can no more solve the environmental crisis than it can end the novel coronavirus pandemic.

As humans who make up so many disparate societies, perhaps we are only still learning to face an existential threat together. We ought to learn fast. Pandemics are likely to increase in number and breadth as the planet warms and humans spread further; both the warming and the scale of today's pandemics are

2. A *New Yorker* comparison of the responses to the spread of coronavirus in New York and Washington states, published April 26, 2020, revealed the efficacy of following scientists over politicians.

products of the rapid urbanization and globalization of human beings, and in both cases, collectively,
we are murderer and victim both. This is a terrifying moral position for individual people who want to
do good but who wreak havoc just by going about the
day. This is as much the case for asymptomatic individuals infecting others unknowingly with COVID-
19 as for people who, without much choice because of
where they live, have to drive a great distance just to
go to work (the American driver is a leading worldwide source of the carbon dioxide emissions that cause
global warming). Most Americans are indeed trapped
spatially into de facto causing harm to the planet.

In any case, among nearly eight billion people the
very thought of effective collaboration sounds silly and
absurdly naïve. And the mortal danger of COVID-19
hasn't disproven this theory. The Chinese premier
failed to adequately contain the virus or properly in-
form the leaders of other nations. The American president willfully ignored the intelligence presented to
him by members of his own administration on the
extent and immediacy of the threat and then, later,
blamed officials of the World Health Organization for
the spread of the disease in the U.S. The Italian president feuded with the head of the Lombardy region
even as cases were increasing exponentially—merely
because the two men represented different political
parties. Just after Brexit, the prime minister of Great
Britain found no avenue for collaboration with the
European Union. But the E.U. also failed to produce

a unifying strategy for its members to cope with the pandemic, while the leaders of Turkey, Russia, Brazil, and Japan calculated that it would be more expedient to downplay the threat. When heads of state finally decided to show support for a unified response behind the U.N.-supported World Health Organization, the United States was not only absent, but the U.S. secretary of state threatened to withhold funding for the W.H.O. permanently.

The failure of cooperation at the political level, however, masks the extraordinary response by individual citizens of every nation, many of whom have endured weeks of grueling quarantine, without personal freedom or pay. At varying points of the pandemic one-third of the human population was forced to stay at home and 90 percent of children away from school. Each person who stays inside, wears a mask outside, and avoids unnecessary social interactions during the pandemic is aligning personal moral responsibility with the broader public good. And, notably for the subject of this work, they are practicing communally for the distinctly dire peril ahead. The neurosurgeon and health reporter Sanjay Gupta said on CNN, "How I behave . . . affects your health. How you behave affects my health. Never . . . have we been so dependent on each other, at least not in my lifetime, and we should rise to that occasion."

The very breakdown of moral choice and action to each individual, aligning the personal with the societal as Dr. Gupta envisions, suggests that we are capable of acting on the climate and ecological crises as well. At the start of 2020, such thinking would have been fanciful given the political barriers to enacting sweeping and systemic changes to human society. As the consequences of human activity on other creatures and Earth systems became increasingly clear these past few years, the distance between individual intent—or even hope for our children and grandchildren's future—and collective reality had become unbridgeable. It was the source of growing existential dread. But the individual response to the novel coronavirus pandemic invites us to believe this distance can be closed. Perhaps, as with the contagion, it is a matter of believing we have no other choice.

a letter with an
unknown destination

> There are always gaps in our sheaf of light; and always
> behind the mysteries which the rays have penetrated
> stand others, still shrouded in darkness.
>
> J. Henri Fabre, *The Sacred Beetle and Others*

My dear future grandchild,

You do not exist; you may never exist. Nevertheless, this letter concerns the measure of your existence, its possibility and its peril. I hope you don't mind. Your parent, whichever of my two children it might be, may be uncomfortable with this speculative exercise. They are students, enraptured by the world in all its strangeness and familiarity, and the truth is you are the farthest thing from their minds.

But I can't say to you, Let's just keep this to ourselves. The possibility and peril of your future world are theirs just the same. It's mine, too, though by the

time the climate has warmed so much that it is substantially destabilized, I will be a very old man. When
you are my age, and I am long gone, global temperatures will have increased another degree and a half
Fahrenheit, or more than three degrees from the pre-
industrial norm, and large parts of the earth may be
uninhabitable.

I did this to you, and so did my parents and grandparents. All the carbon dioxide we felt it necessary to
emit is a down payment on your terror. Your own parents are not innocent.

How did we let this happen? How did we go on
living normally, as we have, even attentively as we
have, and yet without taking action? Many of us have
known, with increasing depth of understanding and
mounting clarity, at least since 2005. That's when
Elizabeth Kolbert's three-part series "The Climate of
Man" appeared, with the stubborn certainty of a preg-
nancy test, in the *New Yorker*. I can still see the three
magazines open to the article on the wooden bedside
table in our old bedroom, exasperating, incomprehensible, unbearable proof. "As best as can be determined," Kolbert wrote in Part One of the series, "the
world is now warmer than it has been at any point in
the last two millennia, and, if current trends continue,
by the end of the century it will likely be hotter than
at any point in the last two million years."

Most scientists and government officials had
known this for several decades. They knew, in exact-
ing detail, by 1969, the year I was born. In 2005, it

may have been too late. We still don't know for sure. Even now, as I write, as new carbon dioxide emissions stabilize, the legacy carbon released by melting glaciers and by logged and burning forests is driving up global temperatures. Should we reduce carbon emissions further, even to zero, it may not matter. The most hopeful assessment, from the United Nations, is that human beings have less than a decade to severely reduce emissions of carbon dioxide and methane in order to preserve some version of the earth as we know it. Despite increasing awareness of the likely consequences, the global political dynamics of this age, characterized by predatory nationalism, corruption, and energy-intensive capitalism, fiercely conspire against any kind of coordinated inter-governmental response at the necessary scale. The most difficult thing for me to accept is that we simply aren't likely to rise above these systemic, and deeply rooted, obstacles.

As I write this, cool, dry air has finally detached the paste of humidity that had stuck to my city for days, at a far, viscous extent of Hurricane Florence, which swelled some rivers in North Carolina to thirty feet. Is there still such a thing as eastern Carolina? Four hundred miles north, today, the balcony doors are open, the house breathing at last, and outside there are footsteps, voices, shallow laughter, but mostly on this quiet night (the eve of Yom Kippur), vehicles passing, grinding internal combustion engines, burning fuel.

We had been warned, you see, but we didn't know how to heed the warning. It's a rule of humanity that our actions are often the very opposite of their intent. We became aware of what we were doing to ourselves and our planetary home, and to you, dear future person, and we thought to ourselves we really must stop. We really must find new, gentler ways to live that won't negate the future. But what have we done instead? Among the many acts of denial, we humans of the early twenty-first century invented something called "ridesharing," which allowed us to grab a ride in an automobile whenever we needed it (and we began, in earnest, to test the self-driving car). At the very moment we intended to do better—reduce emissions, replace the number of private vehicles on the road—the major ridesharing services, according to a study by the transportation expert Bruce Schaller, added 5.7 billion vehicle miles in just nine U.S. urban areas over six years.[3]

Forgive me, my dear, in this present age we turn to data in order to explain ourselves to ourselves. Data tell stories, the researchers and statisticians say, they reveal what we cannot easily see. Perhaps the data are a kind of mirror for the collective soul, but it's about

3. This amounted to more than five trillion pounds of carbon dioxide for the convenience of mostly affluent people, so noted Schaller's study ("The New Automobility: Lyft, Uber and the Future of American Cities," Schaller Consulting, 2018), and at the cost of the use of public transportation and taxis. Ridesharing doesn't replace private vehicles already on the road, it adds substantially more, increasing vehicle miles traveled by 83.5 percent, researchers Alejandro Henao and Wesley Marshall have discovered ("The Impact of Ride-Hailing on Vehicle Miles Traveled," *Transportation*, September 2018).

that injured soul, overwhelmed to the point of despair by the interests of corporations, that I write. It may not be that ridesharing was a bad idea. It was meant to fill a distinct human need using the latest technology. But the hunger of capitalism for money to make more money took over. Overall, the automobile continues to exhaust human and material resources and emit catastrophic levels of carbon dioxide. Far beyond ridesharing, the automobile has spread, an invasive greasy species swarming the earth.

In the United States, this process has been oiled by the Supreme Court, which granted corporations the same right of speech as human beings—a right that critically includes the freedom to speak through lobbying the government for special treatment. Fossil fuel and transportation companies, utilities, and their trade associations spent two billion dollars between the years 2000 and 2016 to convince U.S. representatives and senators to back off writing new laws that would reverse climate change—influence documented in a scholarly paper by the sociologist Robert J. Brulle of Drexel University. Brulle indicated the obvious: this two billion speaks quite a bit more loudly than the whispers of environmental groups or the stutters of concerned citizens outraged enough to call or write their legislators.

This inequality of influence is at the core of our despairing human soul. I hope you understand that, individually and collectively, we humans today don't want to melt the glaciers or hasten the extinction of other species. The problem is the political power we have granted to non-beings, political influence that has perpetuated itself almost exponentially. We created a monster, in other words.

Something else aggravates the despair. I am an individual being in a constellation of associations: friend, colleague, husband, son, father, perhaps grandfather. I am also a citizen, and like many others, I try to be conscientious; I hope above all to be a public-minded citizen. Yet almost incidentally, I am a consumer. All of us are consumers. In that role, we become complicit in harming the ecology of the planet. Here's how: The two billion dollars spent by fossil fuel and transportation companies on lobbying doesn't count the approximately twenty-three billion dollars spent, according to industry observers, on advertising propaganda each year by the American automobile and airline industries (the transportation sector being the single largest U.S. emitter of greenhouse gases that lead to global warming), to sell us relentlessly on the joy of unfettered mobility, the fullest and most divine freedom, self-actualization, and pleasure through unlimited travel, free of costs to human society, personal well-being, or the futures of the nine million other species living on Earth. Each year, this is money spent to ensure our complicity as active and enthusiastic consumers in the burning of carbon-producing fossil fuels. It works two ways, in my calculation. First, the saturation of advertisements has the effect of compromising our capacity to think and act independently and critically about the subject of burning fossil fuels, or any of a dozen other mostly invisible actions that harm the planet. (And no one is running any countering ads, "How about walking to work today?" In the U.S., at least, where only a tiny percentage lives in places where proper pedestrian infrastructure would even make this possible, such an ad would amount to a cruel joke.) Second, the advertising works more directly by helping to close the deal. Your freedom and pleasure are one transaction away. A salesperson's work doesn't matter until a buyer comes along. Consenting to be exploited as consumers (indeed, embracing it), we become exploiters of the earth. In this way, passivity becomes aggression. So inured as we are to living in consumer cultures, we don't even realize we're doing it.

Dear future child, we humans have always believed in the idea of freedom the ad-person's selling, and this makes us especially vulnerable to the pitch. Twenty-three billion dollars a year of propaganda makes easy work of the mind and heart, especially when it confirms a mythic need or at the very least the thrill of the open road portrayed in advertisements for vehicles branded Equinox, Trailblazer, Journey, Explorer, Expedition, Puma, Passport, and Renegade. Few of my generation of Americans, substantially raised in the suburbs, nested in automobiles, thought otherwise. We drove relentlessly, slavishly, to prove everything about ourselves. For my own part, I sank low and pushed the driver's seat back and took off my shoes.

For reasons of self-identity, I drove lazily, straying into the oncoming lane, and sometimes I drove fast. I drove to be with friends and girlfriends, to grant myself space, indeed, to test the limits of freedom. Perhaps the mythic nature of the vehicle best suits the teenage heart. And this is precisely the reason for the trailblazing ads, to convince you the new car will return you to that mythic place, when for most adults a car is an over-torqued tool for practical errands, activities that with a different spatial arrangement mere legs would do. But I don't wish to downplay myth, hardwired as it may be.

Italo Calvino was a twentieth-century writer who, alongside works of profound vision, translated mythic Italian folk tales into modern prose. The careful study confirmed for him the power of the impulse to flight that in my thinking has predisposed us to complicity in the burning of fossil fuels. How else but a motor vehicle or an airplane to propel beyond the everyday? "In villages where women bore most of the weight of a constricted life," Calvino wrote in the first of his *Six Memos for the Next Millennium*,[4] "witches flew by night on broomsticks or even on lighter vehicles such as ears of wheat or pieces of straw." If, as Calvino figured, human beings by nature seek elevation of body and spirit to remedy grim existential reality—"the privation actually suffered," he wrote—then ours is the capacity for vast and immediate mobility to other

4. In the English translation by Patrick Creagh.

places, other lands, to stretch our human settlements as far as possible from the ugliness of poverty, pollution, and pestilence.

To escape, I drove, my friends drove, my parents drove, my grandparents, my uncles, aunts, and cousins. The ancient trees, the vast oceans absorbed all that carbon in silence, as if enduring the irritating noise of terrible children. As if all the while thinking, they know not what they have done.

In other words, dear future person, since self-invention, the archetypal act of American freedom, was so engrained in our spirit, we were willing partners in your most certain suffering. To deny our own complicity in the invasive system of capitalism that has liberalized some human beings but also erased human cultures would be dishonest.

Today we hear the words and witness the actions of a Swedish teenager, Greta Thunberg, who speaks to the powerful as a righteous prophet of future life on Earth, demanding the immediate end to carbon emissions. The sound of her voice is the sound of the voices of the early-nineteenth-century abolitionists, Lucretia Mott and Frederick Douglass and Angelina Grimké and William Lloyd Garrison and Frances Harper: sharpened yet blunt, pointed yet shaking with passion, clear as crystal and yet impossible to hear. It is also, as I imagine it, the voice of you, my grandchild. "You have stolen my dreams and my childhood with your empty words," Thunberg told global political leaders at the United Nations in 2019 after sailing across the ocean on a permanent school strike to demand urgent action to arrest the climate crisis. "And yet I'm one of the lucky ones," she went on.

> People are suffering. People are dying. Entire eco-
> systems are collapsing. We are in the beginning
> of a mass extinction, and all you can talk about is
> money and fairy tales of eternal economic growth.
> How dare you!

Yet many humans can't hear Thunberg's words. Glaciers are calving, forests are on fire, and insects are disappearing; it's as if we know there are bombs going off but we can't hear them. We know what is happening to the planet, but, largely due to the increasing human separation from nature, it hasn't sunk in. Thunberg doesn't yet make sense. Her words must sound to many people as if she had spoken them in another language, about a world they can't quite fathom.

Can you see I'm trying to find my own words to explain our precarious moral state? You must wonder why we didn't act. Perhaps, as it took with abolition, to remove the chains of fossil fuels we'll need a war or revolution. Perhaps by your time that war has happened. We in my present bear responsibility by virtue of knowing, by taking part, merely by witnessing so much of the living earth die.

This is our affliction, and it is intellectual as well as emotional, physical, and spiritual. Recently, a passage in the novel *Compass*, by French writer Mathias

Énard, struck me as speaking to this affliction. "Even if no one had anything to do with this disaster that was all of ours . . . ," Énard wrote plaintively[5] of the destruction of life's infinitude. As I read, I completed the sentence: surely, we all must bear the burden.

The disaster—which you have inherited—is near impossible for us to fathom in its totality. That is one reason for our lack of action. Despite the human brain's great capacity, we are limited by our subjective perceptive power; we can't always reconcile second-hand information with first-hand sensory experiences, especially when life in many respects appears to continue as normal. The disaster is really many linked disasters, some moving at a rapid pace—when a glacier calves it does so with a sudden and final bellow—others in slow motion, one extinction at a time.

But we do sense at least, at the start of the third decade of the twenty-first century, that "It's more than climate change," as scholar Donna J. Haraway wrote in her book of speculative existential futures, *Staying with the Trouble.* Something strange and horrifying is going on, Haraway demonstrated, as she defined the contours of disaster beyond global warming: "It's also extraordinary burdens of toxic chemistry, mining, nuclear pollution, depletion of lakes and rivers under and above ground, ecosystem simplification, vast genocides of people and other critters, et cetera, et cetera, in systemically linked patterns that

5. In the English translation by Charlotte Mandell.

threaten major system collapse after major system collapse after major system collapse."

So many ongoing, interconnected chains of collapse: old growth forests, from Australia to Brazil to Canada, on fire, releasing rather than storing ancient hauls of carbon; the carbon then released acidifying and warming the oceans; marine species, already depleted by overfishing, suffocating to death. And so on, in a vicious cycle of annihilation. Earth's most majestic and abundant ecosystems are vanishing as I write: the Pacific Ocean's Great Barrier Reef now half bleached and therefore depleted of the strength to withstand those increasing ocean temperatures, its 1,500 fish species cut off from the once magical coral home; the river system of the Bío-Bío, once such a great wild torrent that for centuries it repelled Spanish *conquistadores*, now lobotomized by seven hydroelectric dams and left wasted, vacant, and incapable of resisting total collapse of its ecosystem, which will only result in further depletion of the river.

Many scientists say the reality, that is, the environment you inhabit, will be far more depleted of life than it is now. For rising seas and flooding and days and weeks of blistering temperatures and humidity of more than 80 percent and at the same time drought and accelerating desertification are certain to cause political instability, desperation, and war. Severe economic inequality will exacerbate the effects and, without some kind of global revolution, be only further exacerbated. The unraveling of interconnected ecological systems will strain the food supply and send more people (there are already some 65 million today) into some kind of exile. Ah, you know this! I just want you to know we did, too. We have robbed you—your parents, our own children, perhaps, just the same—of the stability that forgiveness requires. You won't have the luxury to grant it. Perhaps you will condemn us instead.

The chapters that follow this letter are an act of struggle; I want you to know I did struggle, and in that struggle I keep searching for words, visions, metaphors, past events, intellectual frameworks, theories, pulses of language from now and any time to help harbor the burden. How to live alongside disaster? You'll find few answers in this letter and in the chapters that follow, and fewer still prescriptions for action. Rather I attempt to construct an existential lattice, a structure for thinking about what is happening from a perspective of moral responsibility and justice. What do we owe ourselves as a species and what do we owe the rest of the living world? What do I owe you?

To think, I read. I keep reading. Énard's melancholic *Compass* leads me to lines from the late Iranian poet Forugh Farrokhzad. From my vantage point, her 1960s work "I Pity the Garden" presents a way to assess the very burden I'm feeling now, of living fully in a dying world. "No one thinks of the flowers," she wrote,

No one thinks of the fish.
No one wants to believe the garden is dying,

that its heart has swollen in the heat
of this sun, that its mind drains slowly of its
      lush memories.[6]

Such a world swollen by heat and drained of memory—what will it require of you? Something quite unbearable, I imagine. I should beg forgiveness, but how could I possibly expect you to be able to forgive? Something perhaps I can't imagine.

I don't wish this to be an exercise in speculation, however. I am bound by now. I'm curious about your world, but hesitant to play games of vision. And this, I confess, is why, beyond all, I ache for you: the loss of privilege to dream, to self-invent, to live free. To elevate above, to move beyond. To be anything, to live anywhere. I fear that by exercising this freedom we have foreshortened yours. We've stolen your future and I grieve for you long before you are even born. In my grief, which is despair over what might have been and will no more, I see a path to melancholy but also the possibility of freedom. You will have to redefine the actions of freedom, if you can. But then the imagined peasant woman of Calvino who conjures a soaring witch on a broomstick to steal her from backbreaking labor wants only to imagine a way out, that a path exists to a more beautiful world. This, I think, when generalized and combined with empathy, is a first murmuring of justice. Perhaps your freedom, sev-

6. Translated by Sholeh Wolpé.

ered from the luxury of pure self-actualization, will expand beyond the personal, perhaps even, as Donna Haraway comes to argue, beyond the human, to create new modes of living with other kinds of living things. As I hardly understand the nature of things today, I may be wrong about everything in 2085, or whatever year you will turn fifty, though it is hard to ignore climate models that, for example, forecast weeks and weeks of additional ninety-plus-degree Fahrenheit days per year. Perhaps melting polar ice unleashes some heretofore unknown system of cooling and the inexorably mounting temperatures begin to falter. Perhaps you discover a new way to exist. Survival probably looks futuristic, at least to my eyes, some kind of final separation of man and nature. I mourn this thought, but who am I to tell you what to do? You won't find any advice here.

Truth is, we leave the balcony doors open much of the time. The rain comes in and warps the floorboards. After a summer of rain, they feel, underfoot, soft as sand. Mold has started growing on the ceiling of the little bathroom—I smelled it several times before I looked up and saw the black spores in the first propulsive stitches of a tapestry. The musk choked me, even to take a pee. We brought your parent up here in this house, your father or possibly your mother, with the windows and doors open. Over the years, the neighbor's gray cat has wandered in, and a yellow bird, and wafts of marijuana, and drumbeats and sirens and giant flies.

We let that world in for a reason. It was the true world and it would be dishonest to deny it. Far be it from us to shelter our children. But the mold in the bathroom: that's the thing, it has to go. The belief that we can't live with the mold, that we have to undertake heroic acts to abolish it, finds favor in science. Black mold can kill. Yet the instinct to destroy the bathroom spores is the same instinct that's created the ecological crisis, the instinct to subdue other living forms for our own benefit. I'm not sure how we reconcile this, either, when it must seem to you, my dear, that because of that instinct everything is out of control.

The poet Farrokhzad wrote,

> I fear the age that has lost its heart,
> the idleness of so many hands
> the alienation in so many faces.

But, she wrote, she won't become alienated from the garden. Love and justice must be possible and through them healing.

> I am forlorn
> and imagine it is possible to take the garden
>   to a hospital.
> I imagine I imagine
> And the garden's heart has swollen in the heat
> of this sun, its mind slowly drains of its
>   lush memories.

Maybe you, too, are sitting in a garden, and though the pond is empty and people scattered in desperation or self-deception, you are there to face it. It gives me joy to think that you might be inclined, as I am, to stick your hands in the earth no matter if it is drained of all memory of what had grown there before.[7] Perhaps the wisdom to dig your fingers inside the body of this dying planet becomes an overpowering instinct toward healing. Our family produces determined people, and no small number who have faced adversity with grace. Among them, like you, I imagine, are seekers of justice.

> With love from the edge of reason,
> Your Grandfather

7. "I will plant my hands in the garden soil," Farrokhzad declared in another poem. This one she called "Reborn."

we are not alarmed

It is not necessary that people be wicked but only that they be spineless.

James Baldwin, *The Fire Next Time*

Things had moved too fast for him. He had not been warned, he had felt the first snatching tug of current, he had seen the skiff begin to spin and his companion vanish violently upward like in a translation out of Isaiah, then he himself was in the water, struggling against the drag of the paddle.

William Faulkner, *If I Forget Thee, Jerusalem*

PARALYSIS

The three things of nature in my childhood were my father's garden, an old Lenape tract called the Five Mile Woods, and the river. The garden pulled me in it because it needed me and I, in turn, desired it because I could shape it—how easily it would relent and become transformed. The Five Mile Woods exerted an opposite power, of strangeness and mystery. It was a kind of impossibility—a tract of land that wasn't zoned for anything; it had no use or owner, no paths or marked trails. The river beckoned me every day, but perhaps lacking imagination I had no idea how to approach it, or reason why I would want to. I wasn't one of the kids who spent Saturday afternoons jumping off the bridge.

But around when I turned fifteen, I started reading the memoirs of the late Supreme Court Justice William O. Douglas. He was just slightly younger than I when he realized he could reach the Cascades from his home in the lowland plains of Yakima, Washington. Those mountains beckoned. They loom over his memoir of his early life, *Go East, Young Man*, appearing "to hold untold mysteries and to contain solitude many times more profound than that of the barren ridge on which I stood." He would "conquer" the mountains—such was the young boy's fantasy. For the next ten years he hiked the wilderness between Mount Adams and Mount Rainier; he came to know every trail, peak, ridge, lake, meadow, and mountain stream. In my teens this seemed to me the way one must live on Earth—to know it in the closest possible intimacy, an ant amidst the anthills. I know only one person who has done this, in the mountains around Lake Tahoe and in the Rockies, where he lives now. This friend, Harmon, understands that the closer you get to something the more you might see.[8] The more

8. I last wrote about Harmon in *Song of the City*, then an explorer of the urban terrain (as a slightly older young man, he went west).

you might see, the more you might know; the more you might know, the more you might recognize you don't know. In other words, the world becomes fuller and more complicated the closer you look.

This is what William O. Douglas discovered when he accepted the "invitation to get acquainted" with the mountains: immersion in the natural world leads to wonder and wonder to respect. And respect required humility. The river, the woods, the mountains—these were part of something much grander than himself. Douglas, the first environmentalist on the United States Supreme Court, understood that to maintain a balance between humans and other beings, we had to be mindful of our power. Should we expend forests and mountaintops and rivers to suit only our own economic needs, we Americans—we humans—would lose our humility. Such a loss would come at a spiritual cost. Subdue nature, or believe you can, and it ceases to emit a meaningful and transformative power. It ceases to be religious and, at the time I started reading Douglas, I wanted it to be religious. I needed to be moved.

I needed to be moved as Douglas was, to act. Love of nature had to be performed; this is a religious notion, too. "I am on my knees, will you have me, world?" wrote Bob Hicok in the poem "Confessions of a Nature Lover." Adoration doesn't hold still or keep silent—it demands response. The hippies made this manifest, and I listened and sang and danced along with my recording of *Woodstock* (I was born that same summer), which I returned to as a form of gospel. Still, today, the *Woodstock* album conjures the spirit of possibility.

Then, the next year, came Earth Day, or Earth Week as it happened in Philadelphia. Allen Ginsberg greeted the crowd on the Belmont plateau in Fairmount Park on April 22, 1970, with "Friday the Thirteenth," a poem he may have written for the occasion. "Earth pollution is mind pollution," the work begins. Ginsberg's voice, in the video recording preserved online, was rabbinic and also cosmic, sardonic and also lyric. He had the eternal presence of a prophet.

Perhaps it was the prophet's certainty that I sought, as an organizer of Earth Day II, twenty years later. With a professor's help we invited Ginsberg back. You can't, or ought not, go back. Instead of a crowd of 50,000 in an open field, a handful came to listen, in a tiny basement classroom. Ginsberg was tortured by the room, perhaps confused, overtaken with the absent regard of someone now distant from his moment in time. I can't recall what he read.

Earth Day II was a sad and sloppy performance of adoration. Protest had no particular power in year ten of Reagan and Bush, as cities no longer had a definitive role in civic life. Protest feeds on the propulsive energy of cities, but those cities, having shed most outlets for public engagement, couldn't produce it anymore. Too many people had left. Decentralization that began in earnest with the Interstate Highway Act of 1956 had worked as a political tactic to diffuse labor union power, particularly, but also representation in Congress. Suburban privilege disguised as intensive apathy settled in. On college and university campuses, disengagement had become a value, a hot pursuit.

What then did I mean to accomplish celebrating Earth Day 1990? Was it the ozone layer or loss of wetlands or the proliferation of trash barges or clear-cutting the Amazon rainforest or the toxicity of lawn chemicals or even the incipient worry over "greenhouse gases" that needed addressing? There was no larger movement underway. So, on our own, we planted trees in a city park, even as our classmates back on campus, acting out a junior year rite of passage called Hey Day, wore Roaring Twenties boater hats, then tossed them in the air and smashed them into the ground. A symbol of blind optimism, these hats were made of some kind of polystyrene foam. In the life of the neighborhood where the tree planting and the hat ritual took place, I'm not sure which act was more presumptuous. Did the park need more trees? Did the neighbors demand them? Had anyone considered their care? I had raised the money for them and organized people to dig the holes, but the scene, in memory at least, soon flooded with foam chunks carried on wind and tossed along by passing cars from campus through the streets all the way to the park. Not caring had been the state religion of the 1980s.

In 1990, it was impossible to discern any change. The afternoon gave way to evening. Plastic foam clung to everything.

The Dow Chemical Company product Styrofoam and other types of polystyrene were ubiquitous back then, and, incredibly, are still used today. American coffee, that thin and bitter black water, would eat through a foam cup like mineral spirits (as a kid I learned never to use one to clean a paint brush). We haven't ever reckoned with the invasion of synthetic chemicals and plastics that, as alien beings, have penetrated every surface of life, the totality of it like an act of contagion.

No land or sea creature is safe. *National Geographic* recently published a photograph of a jellyfish that had ingested the thin plastic pull-tab of a cigarette box wrapper. The words "Phillip Morris International" are easily visible in the photograph of the jellyfish. Right around the time of the collegiate hat ritual, polystyrene foam had emerged as a villain, an easy symbol of mass degradation of the environment precisely because scientists said it wouldn't ever degrade—in a landfill not for a million years. Busted up, it released a bonding agent, chlorofluorocarbon. When emitted en masse, CFCs were burning a hole in the ozone layer, exposing beings to harmful sun radiation.

The philosopher Timothy Morton gave this kind of phenomenon, which exists far beyond our capacity to comprehend, in scale and in kind, a name: hyper-

object. Because it breaks down into infinite particles, unpredictably invading sectors and dimensions
of the biosphere, immediately and then as microns
for thousands or millions of years, all the plastic in all
the world is a hyperobject. And so is global warming.
"Hyperobjects envelop us," wrote Morton in *Hyperobjects: Philosophy and Ecology After the End of the World*,
"yet they are so massively distributed in time that they
seem to taper off, like a long street stretched into the
distance." A single mind can barely conceive it.

In my conception, capitalism is also a hyperobject.
We think we grasp capitalism by virtue of being consumers or investors or workers or entrepreneurs. But
we can't envision, trace, or conceive of the origins of
all the money earning money in all the world going
back to the eighteenth century. Where that money is
going and what it is doing distorts everything about
our lives, but we're not really sure how. Capitalism
pervades every aspect of life on Earth, in elaborate
chains of banking systems, government regulations,
trade deals, markets for securities and markets for
products, supply chains, just-in-time delivery, power
to coerce elected governments, ways of life, philosophical underpinnings of enlightenment notions of freedom, modes of extraction, multinational conglomer-
ation, oligarchical wealth, even philanthropy: we can
list a few elements but can't conceive of the totality.
When I think about it intently, I begin to doubt if I
have any agency or selfhood. Rather it seems to me
I'm merely some kind of highly calibrated machine for

perpetuating capitalism itself. I act on its behalf without ever reflecting on it, even when the action is to my own detriment. It never stops attacking us because it's also inside us.

Hyperobjects are thus fundamentally destabilizing. "Because they so massively outscale us, hyperobjects have magnified this weirdness of things for our inspection: things are themselves, but we can't point to them directly." I am myself, but I can't point to me directly. Not if I wish to take into account family history, genes, DNA, chemical accidents, or the swarm of bacteria who share my being. Morton put it this way: "The gap between phenomenon and thing yawns open, disturbing my sense of presence and being in the world."

Like a predator, polystyrene foam stalked my Earth Day II demonstration. Something truly weird and foreign had invaded the landscape (plastics only existing en masse since the 1950s). My response was to point to what I could see, infinite broken foam particles seeping into newly dug tree pits, indicating injury to Earth, or in keeping with Morton's terminology, that something just wasn't right. This is how in those days I perceived such pollution, or mining, or the filling of wetlands: as predatory acts of the powerful over the powerless. Acts of injustice. The earth, and its beings, had to be protected from mortal injury. It had to be taken, in the words of the poet Forugh Farrokhzad I discovered much later, to a hospital. The instinct to act was thus an instinct of love. The problem has always been to reconcile love, which derives from and demands intimacy, with the inconceivability of living on a large balloon spinning in space, where life is a chemical accident. How is it possible to love a hyperobject?

On Earth Day I had tried, and quite badly failed, to evoke for the public any sort of ecstatic love for Earth. The year 1990 hardly made room for poetry, neither the liberal-minded, sober, mid-century kind of William O. Douglas, nor the liberation poetry of Allen Ginsberg. One felt a broad-scale desiccation. Our lips cracked open and there weren't any jobs. Right-wing assaults on the public sphere intensified. It couldn't be possible to love something like the earth, let alone perform the love. I moved to Michigan, where the twentieth century was pooling in toxic puddles. Far too many people I got to know intimately had cancer. I'd accepted a position as a canvass director for the Public Interest Research Group, the consumer rights and environmental lobby founded by Ralph Nader, and went to work for PIRG in Michigan, one of the oldest chapters. My job was to train canvassers and, on many nights, go with them to knock on doors.

I had a room in a cozy Arts and Crafts house in Ann Arbor, for that well-heeled university town was the location of the main PIRG in Michigan office, rather than the majority poor and African American city of Detroit.[9] Southeastern Michigan was deformed by race, but also class, and class is shorthand for proximity to poison. The people of Flint, seventy miles away, understood this long before the recent drinking water crisis—Michael Moore's *Roger and Me* had spelled it out: the desire for corporate profit meant that labor, like the foam cup, would have to be disposable. People felt disposed all across Michigan, I learned that fall. Capitalism didn't seem to need them anymore.

An environmental canvass runs, in part, on the same mania as a sales office; *Glengarry Glen Ross* meets *Hair*, in effect. Canvassers have quotas to meet each night and goals for signing up members. A thirty-five-dollar member last year might be talked up to fifty this year (though recession often shrunk the thirty-five to twenty, or zero). Stick to your "rap"; get as many names signed on quickly as you can (people are more likely to give if their neighbors have); be personable at the door, but never give up. Get invited in! The canvass director is in charge of assigning turfs, coordinating transportation, and debriefing with each canvasser at the end of the night. At last, like William O. Douglas, I became intimate with the places I walked through. I came to know every expressway,

9. Notably exposing the environmental movement's blindness to race and conveniently excused by the legacy student movement at the University of Michigan. Rodney King had just been beaten by Los Angeles police; that October Anita Hill found herself demeaned and dismissed by a panel of white men.

river, creek, bridge, town, neighborhood, subdivision, diner, dive bar, and Coney Island hot dog joint within an hour of Ann Arbor.

To demonstrate one's dedication to the rest of the crew, a canvass director is expected to take a turf every other night. We go into battle together. Significantly, hitting a nightly quota depends on the director's skill at raising money—often double or triple the amount a staff canvasser can wrangle on a single night. I sat at kitchen tables, on front porches, in tiny vestibules, and gathered checks I stuffed behind the pages of brochures and articles on my clipboard, at the same time gaining new perspectives on fear and justice in Detroit. It was easiest to raise money quickly in the somewhat liberal, and Jewish, neighborhoods of Bloomfield Hills northwest of the city and pleasant to walk around the robber baron cribs along the lakeshore in Grosse Pointe. Aristocrats whose fortunes were made from oil prize the open air most poignantly.

A new General Motors executive class had installed itself and its Cadillacs in Rochester Hills and beyond, in Auburn Hills and unincorporated parts of Oakland County, as far away from Detroit as they could get. When the doorbell rang, they perceived an existential threat and responded appropriately, often with the slam of the door, or a stern "not for us, thanks." As this was a taste of the fierce private-interest politics to come, it might have been wise of me to take account of their anger, half-directed at themselves for not having bought in a gated community where they would be safe from intrusion.

My Michigan friends counseled that auto executives would always be the hardest to convince of the need for stronger regulation to protect the environment. They saw it as a direct attack on their livelihoods. Though they perceived their economic advantage as white-collar professionals as thin, to them that advantage, which has multiplied in the subsequent decades, was really all that mattered. Now, looking back, I recognize the seeds of upper-middle-class resentment against the working class and poor—and all modes of public policy, from public education to environmental and workplace regulations, to protect them—that became the ideological basis of the Tea Party and the presidency of Donald J. Trump. But then my focus was just a matter of convincing people of what was right, at least as I perceived it, an urgency of purpose that drives any campaign forward.

In the fall of 1991, as I remember it, the best turf was downriver, in the bruised towns like Wyandotte, Trenton, and Flat Rock, below the Ford River Rouge plant. In small brick houses, aging factory workers sustained an urge to stick it to the man. The trees were tall, the storefronts empty, and the heavy metals—in the soil, water, and air—poison to living beings. Michigan has more than 6,600 toxic sites. An evening in Trenton, I might collect fifteen or twenty checks, for fifteen or twenty bucks each, written from the agony of disability or cancer on a promise of sol-

idarity and a premise of action. I often finished canvassing early, if I could, and went for a cup of coffee
or something to eat, and I thought about those people and their diminutive brick houses strung along
a curving chain, like a reptile's vertebrae, the fragile
remains of big industry. I'd spent the evening chatting
up skeletons. And they gave!

But what, exactly, did they get for their money?

After a while I returned to the pick-up spot and
drove the four or five other canvassers back to the
office for cashing out and debriefing. The other crews
would filter into the office, and we would announce
high performers and counsel the struggling. Someone
would invariably quit (often in the middle of his or
her turf, only to crouch along the curbstone, smok-
ing, waiting to be picked up one last time). For many
it was hard and unpleasant work that paid poorly, and
sometimes it attracted people who couldn't hold a job.
You had to believe in the cause, but perhaps not too
much. If you did, you might start asking questions
about the legislative initiatives we were touting at the
door. As in a sales office, we deflected most inquiries
from canvassers and rewarded high earners. And during the summer, most memorably, we made sure they
kept partying and hooking up. For these reasons some
people compared the PIRG canvass to a religious
group or a cult.

Retention became its own end, even among us
"senior" staff (I was making an annual salary of
$12,500). I was told during my training, which took

place in Boston, that I was part of a movement toward revolution. No one explained what that meant. At canvass director training we learned first how to raise money at the door. I was handed a rap to memorize and trained, sales-style, doing role-plays. The rap said nothing about revolution. Brought to a 1960s-era suburban neighborhood in Needham, Massachusetts, I rang doorbells and explained the PIRG chapters' success in passing clean water and clean air legislation. In Michigan, we canvassed on a toxic chemical right-to-know bill and always touted the legacy "Bottle Bill," a minor victory for common-sense waste management that gave Michigan the most effective bottle-return-and-reuse system in the nation. But we never asked people to take direct political action; we never connected our work to the specific yet diffuse and complicated legislative mechanisms ongoing in Lansing or Washington. Nor did we campaign as part of larger, broadly situated political movements. In this sense, it was impossible to ignore the distance between the words we were saying and the far-off, perhaps nonexistent, actions those words were meant to describe. Because of the conviction and personal energy needed to knock on the door of a stranger, the distance sometimes felt uncanny. On these fall evenings, Halloween approaching, I first began to sense the futility that would manifest later as paralysis. Out on the turf, reciting the rap, wasn't I merely an actor playing a role? This didn't feel like revolution—more like exploitation of misery.

These multiple overlapping discrepancies diminished my enthusiasm for the campaign. It led to a feeling of ennui and ultimately disengagement. Nothing about what we were doing seemed to add up. Once in a while in Ann Arbor, we would receive notice from Boston that the campaign had changed (by the time I left the organization the PIRG chapters had begun running canvasses for other organizations, including the Sierra Club—it was a kind of profit center). With the notice, we would receive a new rap. One can see how this would make strategic sense—especially if the national organization was working to build support for a bill in Congress. It might take years to pass a new piece of regulation, but to be successful a canvasser had to establish a sense of urgency. She had to believe the cause was urgent, even if, as was certainly the case, the legislation in question wouldn't ever advance out of committee. She had to speak of unreality, to inflate success, to confuse. It didn't matter—it was all for the good of the campaign.

To cover the distance, we pretended to be experts. As director, I went to the store and bought various consumer products that contained toxic chemicals, cancer agents like toluene or benzene. We displayed them on a table and called newspaper reporters and television stations to come see. We handed out a PIRG report—the same one, more or less, year after year—revealing the health consequences of exposure and the danger of weak regulation. Because the campaign was a distant and diffuse construct, the press conference was meant to produce specific evidence: a news clipping or two, with a recent date, that the canvasser could show or hand out at the door. The canvasser was to appear an expert, the organization on the cusp of passing new laws to regulate toxic pollution. Neither was true.

However, this part of the job was a welcome respite from recruiting, interviewing, and hiring canvassers and going out "in the field" every other night knocking on doors. Recruiting and hiring wasn't much different from canvassing. You had to talk fast (and with the utmost certainty), shade the truth, and close as swiftly as you could—before the recruit, or the donor, might change her mind. Because I knew how to write a press release and dial newsrooms to follow up, it was a relief to step out of the canvass and into the real world. In front of the cameras, with containers of toxins in hand—evidence at the scene of the crime—I spoke with conviction. I believed. I still do. An American manufacturer can introduce a new product with an untested chemical compound with utter impunity; it's up to medical researchers, field monitors, and the occasional regulator to document adverse effects. Elsewhere a manufacturer has to prove the compound is safe before it can be sold. How easily in this country we grant freedom to the predator.

I must have made my convictions known to the other members of the PIRG in Michigan senior staff, some of whom I lived with in the turn-of-the-century house a mile from Ann Arbor's downtown. Midwest-

erners are the kindest Americans and the most at ease
with themselves. They understood I was tormented
by the distances between truth and action, between
the urgency of the environmental crisis and the mer-
cenary goals of the canvass. They felt the same way,
only were more capable of laughing at themselves.
I long, even now, to disappear into their tranquility
and quiet. To calm my torment, they recommended
I take part in a regional policy summit along with
PIRG in Michigan's legal director, Andy Buchsbaum,
who today is a vice president of the National Wild-
life Foundation, and representatives from other Michigan environmental advocacy groups. At last, this was
something real. I would learn the geography of pollution and the landscape of political ideology that over-
lay it, the forces that either tried to ameliorate it or
hold it in place. At last, here were the lawyers, policy experts, scientists, and community organizers I
hoped to befriend and support, whose work would
infuse the canvass with the solid and the substan-
tive. I recall a conference room table in a wood-pan-
eled room and stacks of briefing papers on a shelf. I
sat at that table proud of my connection to Andy, who
already in his thirties had won numerous cases against
polluters. That's all I recall—nothing further. Very
soon I was transferred. The Lansing canvass office
was flagging and needed new leadership. Perhaps the
point, in reactivating it, was to prove to lawmakers
that upstate residents were behind environmental regulations. This rationale must have been explained to

me and I must have believed it, but never again was I given the opportunity to take part in the larger work of the campaign. I rented a large, tattered apartment on a desolate block just behind the state capitol. It was winter now.

With only old boxes of member records, the office had to be started from scratch. I recruited canvassers at Michigan State and found a small, second-floor office adjacent to campus. The furniture was found, or donated—each PIRG office was a *Mad Men* museum. A canvasser named Masha told me that in Russian my name meant "tush." I hired a soybean farmer who needed work in the winter and, every day, I ate a burrito for lunch. I started composing a novel about a lost suburban family. At night I called in my daily numbers to Ann Arbor. It occurred to me I'd once written an essay, for an application to college, about the false positivity of Willy Loman in *Death of a Salesman*. How I'd despaired for the man who had to fabricate hope in order to survive. The PIRGs never shook the cult comparison in part because they enforced such a denial of the facts on the ground. Running a canvass in February in Lansing, Michigan, during a deepening recession was damned near impossible. But who should be allowed to admit it? At night, I cooked some pasta, lay on the futon in my inconceivably large bedroom, and watched rented movies. I had imagined the purpose of my work was to convince lawmakers and regulators to protect the earth and its creatures from injustice. The capitol dome was right out my window—I never pulled the shades. Nevertheless, it seemed impossibly far away.

After Lansing, I became canvass director in Columbus, Ohio, and then Philadelphia. Today, I can't name a law or a new regulation or rule I helped get approved, if, in fact, there were any. It might be easier to calculate how much money I helped raise, but for what? A million checks catching the wind, so many written with earnest intent (and others to get rid of the intense guy at the door). Having no discernible impact, I got bored. I went back to school to try something else. The distance between intent and action, between the predatory assault and our capacity, or even desire, to respond, seemed impossible to breach.

Today, the distance has shifted and taken a new, more powerful form, causing not only frustration but also paralysis. The Styrofoam still clings to everything—the metaphor is simultaneously real. A mere glance at the news this morning before I started writing, no more than forty-five seconds, revealed rising tides pulling Scottish historic sites into the sea, Antarctic lichen dying from heat, and the substantial and demonstrable ecological destruction of American national parks, warming at twice the rate of the planet. These reports are random messages from the hyperobject global warming, words that we point to that represent distant phenomena that we understand to be real. One might even travel to Scotland or Antarctica or Yellowstone and with the right equipment document these changes for oneself.

Yet the data, transforming the real into abstract measurements, distance us still further, as if our attempt to grasp global warming only pushes it away. In the U.S. there are many difficult problems we can wrap our minds around: poor access to health care, over-incarceration, refugee child internment, inadequate public transportation, police brutality against Black men, lack of education funding, school loan debt, crumbling infrastructure, gender discrimination, incessant gun violence, mass opioid addiction, even historic levels of income inequality; these problems captivate us for hours because they are present and real in our lives, because we can conceive of their dimensions beyond abstract data, and because we understand how, specifically, to solve them (even if the political will is yet to develop). But faced with the hyperobject of global warming, I find, we can't even hold a conversation for two or three minutes before someone, unable to conceive of the primordial reality let alone the consequences, changes the subject. It is almost impossible not to look the other way. The cause of the paralysis is in part the incapacity to grasp something so diffuse in cause and effect. But it is also, I argue, a matter of complicity.

COMPLICITY

In evoking the dimensions of paralysis, I have been using the first-person plural quite consciously and purposely, hoping to straddle the conflicted space between the individual's responsibility and her part in the collective. But "we" is indeed slippery. The word masks critical differences among human beings, ignores the dispersal of choice and action, and can't account for degrees of power in and across societies. This lack of uniformity is one more cause of paralysis.

Who, exactly, bears responsibility? Who are "we"? The Qatari prince with six jets and three wives? The Cameroonian refugee who plays songs to forget (and never forget) the atrocities he escaped? The Indian village girl who walks ten miles to school? The ethnic Vietnamese mother who sells food she prepares to neighbor families living in floating houses on Tonle Sap in Cambodia? The woman who lives in a one-hundred-square-foot apartment in Shenzhen and assembles iPhones? The Icelandic airline steward? The head of Gazprom? The Xfinity service man who replaces your router? The fifth-generation Puglian winemaker who flies all over Europe and the U.S. giving free tastings of his family's vintage? The indigenous man who takes payments from shady diamond miners and loggers for access to the rainforest? The American general contractor who recommends mahogany for your outdoor deck? The Mexican immigrant who goes through six dozen Styrofoam takeout containers each day at her taqueria in St. George, Utah? The Kenyan coffee bean picker in line for the morning ration? The grandmother from eastern Turkey forced to move to Istanbul because her son-in-law can get a job in a T-shirt factory on the outskirts of the city (which consumes its outskirts and forms new ones each half-year)? The Istanbul fixer who finds the family an apartment on a hill where sheep grazed only yesterday? The Romanian novelist who falls in love with an Argentinian poet at a literary festival in Oslo? The Israeli tech executive on the phone with a venture capitalist in Melbourne? The Berlin boy wandering through the forest dreaming of living among the trees forever?

A single mind can't conceive of the vast web of human life or even be aware, with any meaningful precision, of her or you or that woman over there. When we say, therefore, "we must" reconceive our relationship as a species to other living creatures and Earth, we need to consider how much we don't fully understand about what motivates other people to act. Nor do we comprehend the exact consequences of those not fully understood actions—be they elections or inventions, vendettas or social movements.

Nor can we conceive of the complicated networks and layers of human governance. In the United States alone there are 50,000 discreet governing bodies, from school districts to city councils, state assemblies to county commissioners, sewer districts to the Congress of the United States, each making decisions, at relative scale and influence, over the allocation of resources and the regulation of human behavior, and often, given the wide range of political and economic ideologies, at cross-purposes.

The web is vast, but at the center we might place the top executives and trustees of humanity's largest fossil fuel, chemical, automobile, arms, and aviation companies and the government regimes that in various ways enable them. Perhaps these amount to several thousand of nearly eight billion humans: they are our human heart of darkness. They cause war, habitat destruction, and uncontrollable emissions. They also exploit the vulnerability of the two billion poorest humans.

By the year 2050, researchers at the World Bank predict, 143 million people in sub-Saharan Africa, Southeast Asia, and Latin America will be exiled from their homes because of fire, flood, and drought caused by global warming. The mass exile, starvation, and most certainly violence, as well as the disruptions to children's development and education—all this human suffering has a single origin: the unregulated extraction and burning of fossil fuels. Those who sit at our web's center, who hold the power to slash emissions and remove poisonous toxins and invasive extraction infrastructure, bear the most responsibility, and, if they fail to act after recognizing the consequences, the most blame. In a tribunal their victims would have the right to bring them before a judge.

In that imagined tribunal, I suspect that petrochemical executives and their public sector colluders would claim, with a mountain of exculpatory evidence, that they acted reasonably given the rules of political economy, capitalism, national security, and public interest. And besides, they would continue, they weren't the only ones who failed to act. The most vituperative might point to the great benefit to humankind of cheap energy derived from fossil fuels. Many of these people have tried to hide the evidence of responsibility; few concede the urgency of crisis. Only a tiny fraction has developed plans to act.

Not facing known and well-understood acts of destruction may be the moral failure of our time. I wonder if this is a new manifestation of the banality of evil. Hannah Arendt invented the term to account for the manufactured naiveté of the Nazi Adolf Eichmann, whose war crime tribunal in 1961 she witnessed and then interpreted in a five-part *New Yorker* series (and later the book derived from it), "Eichmann in Jerusalem." There is a reason I imagined the tribunal: this form of justice has been utilized effectively before.

Eichmann was uniquely responsible for the removal of Jews from Germany via genocide and yet couldn't account for his actions except to admit to following orders. Or not. It didn't matter because as a German he had self-canceled his agency; being German was enough.

"Eichmann needed only to recall the past in order to feel sure that he was not lying and that he was not deceiving himself, for he and the world he lived in had once been in perfect harmony," Arendt wrote in the first article in the series, which appeared in 1963. In our day, scholar Donna J. Haraway's book *Staying with the Trouble*, which examines the moral dimensions of living during climate change, invites a comparison of present-day humans with Eichmann and his cohorts. Eichmann, Haraway writes, "could not make present to [himself] what [he was] doing." He could look at what he'd done but could not see. He was unwilling and unable to face it. Nothing could startle his consciousness.

Arendt put it this way, assessing the German culture of complicity: "Eighty million Germans had been shielded against reality and factuality by exactly the same self-deception, lies, and stupidity that had now become ingrained in Eichmann's nature."

Or, as Primo Levi expressed in his harrowing memoir of Auschwitz, *If This Is a Man*: "The Germans are deaf and blind, encased in an armor of obstinacy and willful refusal to know."[10]

And so the web extends. How many more of us— far beyond the narrow set of fossil fuel, automobile, arms, chemical, and aviation executives—shield ourselves by self-deception? What about the lower ranks of these companies, the engineers, the data scientists, the marketing professionals? What about other giant multinational companies, like Amazon and Apple, whose business practices depend on extraction and petrochemicals? Amazon employees, recently organizing to force management to prohibit fossil fuel companies from using their company's cloud-based data services, think the web extends to them. In their well-publicized campaign, they admit to their com-

10. In the English translation by Stuart Woolf.

pany's complicity, and therefore their own. They can't stand to bear the moral weight, even if they share it with the company's billions of consumers. This example suggests that the web of complicity might then stretch far and wide, to include the two to three billion or so human beings who are wealthy enough, as consumers, to contribute overwhelmingly to the ecological crisis.

We among those two to three billion may not share the same level of direct responsibility as Arendt's 80 million Germans. But we are practicing a similar form of self-deception. The German people, who destroyed themselves in their complicity, warn us now: that self-deception is a matter of our existential peril.

The Israeli tribunal that tried Eichmann convicted and hanged him for destroying a third of the Jewish people on Earth. Though he and other Nazi officers participated in the mass burning of evidence toward the end of the war, the facts were more than ample to prove him personally culpable. Yet he wouldn't have been so successful at Jewish removal if millions of others hadn't complied. As Arendt famously wrote, "The trouble with Eichmann was precisely that there were so many like him, and that the many were neither perverted nor sadistic but were, and still are, terribly and terrifyingly normal."

From the viewpoint of our legal institutions and of our moral standards of judgment, this normality was much more terrifying than all the atrocities put together, for it implied—as had been said at Nuremberg over and over again by the defendants and their lawyers—that this new type of criminal, who is indeed *hostis generis humani*, commits his crimes under circumstances that make it well-nigh impossible for him to know or to feel that he is doing wrong.

Isn't this how we commit our crimes: in the most terrifyingly normal way? We of those two to three billion who are just wealthy enough to cause planetary destruction merely by rising in the morning and going about the day—by the simple fact of being alive. As much as complicity in the Holocaust struck Arendt as a new kind of crime to consider from a standpoint of personal moral responsibility, mass ecological destruction and death caused by the quotidian interconnected actions of a vast range of human beings strikes me as still more vicious. We are the most slippery kind of criminal.

Levi, in *If This Is a Man*, evokes the terror of Auschwitz wrought by the willfully blind and the stupid who performed their duties with acute precision and efficiency. Selection day came regularly to the barracks of Auschwitz, as Levi recounted. Men lined up in the quartermaster's office, every one naked and holding a card with his name on it. In the time it took for each prisoner to walk past the SS officer, the officer decided if the card should be handed to the soldier on his left or right (so thoroughly was every German complicit). After the lineup, the men returned to the barracks. Left or right, right or left, it wasn't clear which side signified amnesty (for then) and which side death—by gas chamber the day after tomorrow. Left or right? Timothy Morton writes of hyperobjects that they "invoke a terror beyond the sublime, cutting deeper than conventional religious fear."

The men of Barrack 48 looked around at each other. The oldest, sickest, most infirm: did their cards go left or right? This was the only way to guess, to know if condemned that night you could dare ask for a double ration. "If you wound the body of a dying man, the wound begins to heal, even if the whole body will die within a day," Levi wrote. If you feed a condemned man his hunger may begin to quell, Levi observed, but he'll be dead in hours anyway. Levi's card went right; his gruel was gratefully thin. Physical strength impressed the deputized SS officer, but the decision on selection day was ultimately arbitrary: the quartermaster was commanded to eliminate a certain number of men "according to a fixed percentage" to make room for more. The card for a burly peasant from Transylvania who was abducted from his home twenty days before, Levi observed, went left for no apparent reason; the man had no idea what was going on. (I often imagine the terror of animals whose territory, unbeknownst to them, is all of a sudden under attack by bulldozer, chainsaw, fire, dam, and pesticide. They can sense predation but cannot figure it.) After selection ended, the peasant stood in the corner of the barrack and mended his shirt. Kuhn, an older man, sat on his bunk and prayed thanks to God his card had gone right. "Does he not see, in the bunk next to him, Beppo the Greek, who is twenty years old and is going to the gas chamber the day after tomorrow, and knows it, and lies there staring at the light without saying anything and without even thinking anymore?" Levi wrote of Kuhn's blindness.Does Kuhn not know that next time it will be his turn? Does Kuhn not understand that what happened today is an abomination, which no propitiatory prayer, no pardon, no expiation by the guilty—nothing at all in the power of man to do—can ever heal?

The terror of Auschwitz cut deeper than conventional religious fear. It could not—it could never—be conceived on standard moral grounds. "If I were God," Levi ended the story of selection day, "I would spit Kuhn's prayer out upon the ground." The inconceivability is part of what makes something a hyperobject, ungraspable. Museums of the Shoah try to ground the impossible by telling specific stories, giving names, exhibiting material evidence. But at the same time the museums try to preserve a sense of the poisoned darkness. How else to indicate why it must be remembered?

Fascists and white supremacists exploit that horror, too—cynically, to justify their hate. Something so repellent, they taunt, could only be made up. This is how denial of the atrocity ends up preserving it, and it becomes a stain that can't be removed. "Hyperobjects," Morton wrote, "do not rot in our lifetimes." This is a stench that endures.

In that sense, an overpowering irrational hatred of Jews, or of any specific group of people, is a hyperobject. The hatred is like a circle of black mold spores: it clings, it spreads, it spirals until it makes us sick.

Yet the Holocaust began and it was ended. British, French, Russian, and American forces destroyed the SS. Allied intelligence officers exposed the intricate systems of murder. Historians still debate what guilt other nations bear, how much they contributed to the genocide, but legal tribunals convicted Nazi war criminals; Eichmann was exposed and hanged. Nazi officers' children and grandchildren and survivors' children and grandchildren of survivors were born, and live, still, in peace.

The ecological crisis, emerging as it has been for decades, and revealing its ultimate and savage horror gradually and intermittently, has no such finite shape. Quite a few scientists and policy makers want to give it shape by calling this period of man's apparent domination of the earth—significant enough to be recorded in the material fabric of the earth's crust—the Anthropocene. "Anthropocene" simultaneously conveys this material infestation and accounts for complicity. It says, whoever broke it should fix it.

But like many labels, "Anthropocene" masks more than it reveals. The dynamic and interconnected systems unraveling—global warming, mass extinction, drought, glacial calving, coral bleaching, and deforestation, among many other examples of human-caused ecological stress—have bolted from our pen and beyond our control. This is one reason to oppose the use of "Anthropocene," which suggests that if we take our responsibility seriously enough, we will be able to herd them back in. The opposite is most certainly, and devastatingly, the likely case.

Global warming is a hyperobject both from the inside of it, where it escapes our control and comprehension, and from the outside. From there, we can't imagine the scale or make sense of what transformations it will produce. Actions like the inadequate half-step of the Paris Treaty, with its inherent belief in the effectiveness of liberal political institutions, place humankind in the dynamic of 1938 (the time of Neville Chamberlain's appeasement of Hitler) and promote the dream that, despite our hapless shortsightedness, the Allies will still one day save us. But by driving and flying and grilling and logging and buying and showering and shipping and tweeting away, we are the Allies and we are the Axis both, in constant, blasé warfare that's leaving us paralyzed at the edge of certain apocalypse.

We are the SS officer making the decision left or right, and also terribly and terrifyingly we are the normal citizens of the Nazi regime and poor Beppo the Greek, the fool Kuhn and even Primo Levi, who never could escape. We are next in line, or our children or grandchildren are, even if we think God will answer our prayers and give us the power or luck to find higher ground. Another way to put it: paralysis is a con game and we are conning ourselves.

Once in a while, in conversation, I try to make this case. It's usually met with silence or the throwaway, "So, then you think we should go back to living in caves?" Perhaps, I mutter. I try to look the person in the eyes. The gaze can't be met. Neither of us will allow it. I press my eyes to the sky instead. Shake the head. Skip the subject. It isn't difficult. Conversation lands anywhere else, both guilt and relief conspiring. The guilt is enough, isn't it, to confirm the thesis? It's not like any one of us matters, the other person might say, after some time goes by, perhaps not wishing to appear indifferent, callous. If you live in a cave, so what? It won't end global warming, as quarantining during the COVID-19 pandemic in 2020 proved.

There are alternative consequences to consider, I might say if the conversation goes this far. Morton wrote that "hyperobjects seem to force something on us, something that affects some core ideas of what it means to exist." The hyperobject global warming forces us to inhabit a conflicted and painful moral space, where we commit harm to other living beings but ignore both the injury and its consequences for purely practical reasons, for matters of convenience. Or perhaps because it's too much to bear. It strikes me as good common sense to say that my personal actions to curb harm are useless, and data bear it out. The carbon I emit is inconsequential. But I can't let go of the existential question forced on us when we live as we do, as if our very way of life weren't causing harm. Who gives us the right?

If we can't live any other way, then perhaps we aren't living but rather slowly killing ourselves. We're ceding the possibility of a moral basis for human society and, simultaneously, through aggressive and unregulated consumption, accelerating its demise. Most certainly, we're individually and collectively privileging our own desire for comfort and wealth over the needs of future generations. I believe it is our moral duty to leave the earth in better condition than how we found it and we have demonstrably failed.

"my cry of alarm"

An immense life force, slow to move, but awesome in its naked power, rouses the stupendous body of the earth, flows over her valleys and knolls, folds her flatlands, bends her rivers, and builds up her thick coat of soil and vegetation. In no time, to avenge herself she'll haul me up to the sky where the skylarks lose their breath.

Jean Giono, *Hill*

AWARENESS

Midway through writing this book I left the city and drove three hours north (along my beloved river) to a village where I took part in a literary festival. After my literary duties, I decided to stay a few days at a house on a nearby lake that my wife's family had purchased almost fifty years ago. The lake was formed by damming a section of the Flatbrook Creek in the 1920s. Small lots were sold for hunting shacks. This one was probably built in the 1930s, perhaps reusing stones from an earlier farmhouse. I come here, as others have before me, to lose the city, its shouting people, aggressive machines, and time schedules, and find instead other, nonhuman, things, to press closer to them, to acknowledge the sky and the wind and ground. One way I become calm and also gently stirred is to kayak to the end of the lake and rest for a while, floating. I follow the flight path of the red-winged blackbirds in and out of the trees. Find the bubbles that lead to the croaking frogs. Fixate on a sunbathing stinkpot turtle. Turn to watch a great blue heron stretch its dinosaur wings on a rock nearby. A trail from the end of the lake penetrates a state forest and connects to state wilderness preserves and a National Park Service recreation area beyond. It is not unusual to spot an eagle or encounter a bear.

It was October. That summer I had never made it to the lake house. Now, when I arrived after leaving the literary festival, I found two-foot-high nimblewill, which spreads by endless highways of roots, choking the perennial beds I had been cultivating for almost two decades. Giant mauve plumes of zebra grass towered over the lake edge, crowding out the red bee balm and blue wild bergamot I've worked so hard to nurture. Deer had eaten dozens of astilbe heads. Jewelweed defied the giant swamp-loving ligularia I had planted, a perennial known as "the rocket." Virginia creeper had shot up to the highest windows. Caterpillars had clear-cut through the leaves of the three cranberry viburnum bushes, including the one I'd managed to resurrect after beavers had absconded with most of its branches years ago. The viburnums' blood-filled berries should have been resplendent, but there were none. In human absence, mallards and wood ducks had squatted the boat docks and left a craggy landscape of scat. Snakes slithered in the zebra grass ahead of my footsteps. Remains of a bass, treat for bird or bear, rotted in the sun. Inside, hairy patches of mold covered an old dresser. A smoldering odor emitted from a dead, hidden mouse. Slime had needed hardly any time to lacquer the porch.

How could I live with such savage decadence? Without much of a thought I began a retaliatory assault, first inside the house. I opened windows, found the mouse and tossed it into the leaf litter beneath the trees. The dehumidifier we'd installed in the lakeside bedroom had gone off. This was the cause of the mold growing on the dresser. I emptied the pan, turned the dehumidifier back on, and wiped the mold from the rosewood drawers. The lakeside garden had to be pruned, overgrown vines ripped down, and all the beds weeded. Even in autumn, with dormancy lurking, I ballooned with need—to rescue the garden from profligacy.

There were still at least a dozen spray cans of pesticides and weed killer in the basement, emblems of my in-laws' approach to the outdoors: nature had to be restrained to be enjoyed (and enjoy it they did, with a slide, various boats, floating chairs with cup holders, and cocktail hour). I'd started building the lakeside garden in 2000, a bright cold April day. The idea was to return it to nature: cut beds for native wild-flowers and grasses into the small lawn and establish a natural transition from land to water—connect the house, an imposition on the forest, to its surroundings. I wanted to return to some less tacky state and to restrain the human instinct to colonize every inch available. Rather than reflect our less subtle instincts, the garden would represent our most calming and quiet ones.

There was a sharper ideology at play in my in-laws' garden as well, related to those spray cans of poison: when we've succeeded in making nature distinct from us, it becomes easy to control, injure, or kill. This is a speculative notion—but one perhaps confirmed by the actions of Mr. Eichmann. The first step to jus-tify genocide is to dehumanize the group you want to eliminate by associating them with elements of na-ture. Call them filthy animals or vermin, or name them savages (European colonizers of North America called the people already living there by this name for a reason). This is precisely why it is alarming for the president of the United States to label immigrants in a similar way. It is also why we can associate environ-mental destruction with genocide—both are enacted to further separate humans from other, more base and repugnant beings.

Attacking the garden that fall, I came to recog-nize that I wanted the lakeshore in front of the house to feel naturalistic, which wasn't the same as natural.

The natural state, after some five months of uncontrolled verdure, wasn't acceptable. Standing on the lake's edge, my fingernails jammed with dark earth, I'd weeded myself into a philosophical hole. To achieve the natural, I'd murdered piles and piles of nature.

It may be no accident that Rachel Carson began writing about the worlds of nature in 1941, the age of genocide. In *The Edge of the Sea*, a book published in 1955, she observed, of life in that daily shifting space, the water's edge,

> Nowhere on the shore is the relation of a creature to its surroundings a matter of a single cause and effect; each living thing is bound to its world by many threads, weaving the intricate design of the fabric of life.

Timothy Morton, inventor of the useful term *hyperobject*, says that if it's possible for us humans to see ourselves as a part of (and not apart from) this fabric, which he evocatively calls "the mesh," the individual inside nature and nature inside the individual, there's no going back. Morton says that the mesh will free each of us from the exhausting fiction of "I." Ultimately, I'll stop trying so hard to control the garden.[11]

When I disappear, my point of view is no longer mine. Being part of everything in this way is both

11. There is difficult circular logic to this claim, which I'll leave be for now. But Morton argues that if a person imagines he is part of the mesh of nature, then anything he does, even suppressing or killing nature, is natural.

humbling and elevating, which makes it a spiritual point of view, a new kind of fervency. So why bother with all those acts of separation? They'll only exhaust you. Just relax instead, Morton says, the world is symbiotic. Accidental bacteria in the gut give us life. Explosions of calcium two billion years ago gave fish their bones. Those bones evolved into our skeleton.

But we have trouble relaxing because the beings with whom we share our bodies are strange and frightening. "We literally host all kinds of beings that flip from friend to enemy in a moment—that's what having an allergic reaction is all about," Morton wrote in *Being Ecological.*

> Symbiosis, which is how lifeforms interconnect, is made up of all kinds of uneasy relationships, where beings aren't in total lockstep with one another.

More troubling, perhaps, the totality of the mesh remains beyond consciousness, too slippery to comprehend, too unwieldy to figure, our own reactions and interactions, choices and instincts too dispersed to put a finger on (where exactly do we fit?). So, we fall back on controlling what's before us on our own miniature earths, as I did in the garden almost without thinking. We build makeshift dikes (or massive engineered ones), we toss lawn fertilizer, spray weeds, arrange plantings, set traps, cast lines, sow, cultivate, harvest, prune, fence—we spend trillions to subdue the very thing that made us possible, most certainly subduing the wildness in ourselves. The billions of human beings whose lives are tied immutably to the land—who farm for subsistence, who live in the rainforest, who get in a tiny wooden fishing boat each morning—subdue the earth directly a thousand times a day just to survive. Many of them dream of not having to do the subduing day in and day out, of living instead in a world where man and nature have already been effectively separated.

We know this separation as modernity—it means we don't have to do the subduing with our own hands.

THE TWO SIDES OF MODERNITY

Modernity, or separation of humankind from nature, is the basis for education, for inoculation, for the engineering of water systems, for rural electrification. Modernity taken too far ends with elimination, mass extinction caused by global warming and man-made pollution. Modernity is destruction and hope all at once, conflicting impulses with which we humans have never reckoned. Now it is very likely too late.

The conflict alone deepens our paralysis. Modernity as destruction suggests the solution is to return to old ways, embrace a more traditional relationship with nature. "Back to nature" is a powerful, enduring urge in people tired of tall buildings, deafening machines, overcrowding, processed food, social media, and pesticides in their water. The need for nature seems primordial, for the savage world is the greatest teacher of time and pleasure; at times it is easy to believe the wind is speaking to me individually, the immutable voice of a god of the elements secreting night and day, dusk and dawn. Back to nature as a political concept, however, is fantasy, because, like all reactionary movements, it imagines a world that never existed and never could exist: pure, simple, and harmonious. Nature's prevailing processes are contamination, predation, disharmony, and adaptation, not stasis or perfection. In the political realm, as the rise of far-right nationalist parties around the world is teaching us, fantasy leads to trouble because it speaks to despair.[12]

Modernity as hope, on the other hand, suggests we should only ever look forward, use human ingenuity, technology, and infrastructure to solve problems of ecology that are both natural, such as malaria, and human-made, such as logging of rainforests. Lab scientists developing plastics from plant materials or building materials from mycelium are performing modernity as hope.

Unlike the fantasy of back to nature, modernity as hope is a basic, functional concept of individual life lived on Earth. It is also a dream: for centuries peasants have migrated to cities for opportunity. In our time this mass migration has transformed Nigeria, Turkey, and China most powerfully, but nearly everywhere on Earth, from Afghanistan to Zimbabwe, has witnessed the change. There is no denying the urge

12. At the same time, the far-right nationalists of our time do not advocate "back to nature," except when they argue that white supremacy is the natural order of things.

for opportunity, comfort, and status that cannot be obtained in a village. But modernity as hope is also a horrifying personal fantasy for billions of humans who live in ad hoc conglomerations of metal shanties at the edge of cities, or near trash dumps, whose children work in dark factories or get sold into prostitution, who drown trying to reach a promised land.

Modernity as hope, as a political concept, is thus a kind of sham perpetrated on poor countries by the rich ones, whose bankers and corporate chiefs enrich themselves on the suffering. According to the liberal market forces at play, someone must always profit from investment; otherwise there is no justification for it. That profit, if history is a guide, is rarely painless for the least protected members of society.

The two imperfect forces, modernity as destruction and modernity as hope, locked in a deadly embrace, have twisted us deeper into a kind of paralysis from which we can't escape. With modernity simultaneously the cause of our problems and our only basis for a solution, the ecological crisis intensifies. In the Amazon rainforest of northwest Brazil, the Paiter Suruí indigenous people had lived without interaction with Europeans until 1969, adapting with the flora and fauna of their forest home for thousands of years. European contact inevitably brought disease, eviscerating the Paiter Suruí population, which dropped from 10,000 to 240. Lumber mills and ranchers moved in. Government policy encouraged economic growth (and return on investment) at all costs.

Facing possible extinction from modernity as destruction, Almir Suruí, the dynamic Paiter Suruí leader, appealed to modernity as hope to save his people's forest home. In 2007 he convinced the engineers behind Google Earth to create a means for tracking and reporting forest loss. The audacity of the project gave the Paiter Suruí enough notoriety to take the upper hand in the fight, and the tool engaged young members of the tribe in the work of progress. The larger challenge was to permanently protect the rainforest while providing an economic alternative to logging or ranching (and for the young people a reason to stay in the village). Collaborating with various international organizations, Suruí enrolled the rainforest in the United Nations-sponsored REDD+ program, a marketplace for carbon credits. A corporation needing to offset its carbon dioxide emissions would pay the Paiter Suruí to maintain and enhance the rainforest as a carbon sink.

Almir Suruí wasn't entirely at ease embracing modernity as hope so nakedly. "I was well aware that our Mother Earth was not supposed to follow the rules of the economic markets and that the REDD+ project was not going to be a perfect solution," he wrote in a memoir co-authored with Corine Sombrun, *Save the Planet*. "But even if our Suruí carbon project wasn't perfect, it was nevertheless going to contribute to an awakening of consciences by demonstrating it was possible to generate profits from the rainforest without destroying it!" The cosmetics company Natura purchased 120,000 metric tonnes of credits from the Suruí and others followed, including the 2016 Rio Olympic Committee.

For a time, it seemed as if Almir Suruí's plan would work. The program enabled the Paiter Suruí to establish education and reforestation projects to heal damaged parts of the thousand-square-mile forest where Almir Suruí was raised and was taught by his father, "The forest is a living thing, and she will only respect you if you respect her."

Yet there was no way, in the Brazilian Amazon, so exposed to the harshest elements of the ecological crisis, to avoid the deadly embrace between modernity as hope and modernity as destruction. A market-based initiative, the Paiter Suruí carbon offset credit project became the target of a powerful Catholic Church–backed indigenous group, CIMI, whose leaders attacked the project as commodification of nature. Though they had the same goal to save the rainforest as Almir Suruí, the CIMI activists saw the project squarely as an example of modernity as destruction, the wealthy earning on the backs of the poor.

The project now weakened by heightening protest, a rival leader, Henrique Suruí, accused Almir Suruí of corruption. Henrique Suruí began making deals with illegal loggers who bribed him and his backers for access to the rainforest. Then miners discovered gold and diamonds in the ground beneath the forest. The result was a free-for-all.

On October 13, 2016,[13] Almir Suruí issued a panicked call for help. "This is my cry of alarm, please listen to me!" he wrote to national and international authorities and environmentalists. "We are undergoing a total invasion of deforesters and miners of diamonds and gold." Each day 300 trucks entered and left the forest filled with lumber, the bounty of nearly 1,500 acres of tropical rainforest. The situation was dire: "Either one collaborates, or they put a gun to our heads!"

As chainsaws effectively weakened the forest's capacity to store carbon, Suruí rightly worried the offset program might collapse. A slashed forest stores less carbon, and as it degrades and sheds biomass, it releases the carbon it had absorbed: in 2017, according to *National Geographic*, some 7.5 million metric tons of it, 50 percent more than the U.S. energy sector emitted that year. In all, Brazil's Amazonian tropical forests lost more than 20 million acres of tree cover to logging, fire, and hurricanes in 2016 and 2017, accounting for one-quarter of the globe's record forest depletion to that point.[14]

The erasing of billions of trees is a slippery kind of hyperobject. The scale of loss can't be conceived at once, nor the specific individual effects on people,

13. Well before the election of an aggressively anti-indigenous-rights figure, Jair Bolsonaro, as Brazilian president.

14. These records were subsequently shattered by the fires of 2019 and 2020, and deforestation accelerated during the COVID-19 pandemic, as regulatory enforcement was curtailed.

birds, amphibians, insects, nor the impact on the tangle nests, spawning grounds, migration patterns, food chains, the entire mesh in which "each individual is necessary," as Suruí wrote, "where each root of each plant deserves to be protected for the harmony and good of all."

In his cry of alarm, Almir Suruí was trying to seize the world's attention, to make us act—immediately—while it was still possible to define the exact nature of the crime. The gun is at all our heads, he said. You living in comfort haven't yet heeded the warning, so let me repeat it. He wrote, "The implications are terrible. In addition to environmental damage (and the challenge to our way of life), these invasions directly endanger our families and our children."

> On behalf of the Suruí people and of all indigenous people who are trying to protect the Amazon rainforest, in the name of our struggle to preserve a future for all children of this planet at the price of our lives, in the name of hope for the future, we ask you to distribute this letter to all your contacts in the world and on social networks, because today we are all connected in a common destiny.

Did anyone outside of the relatively small community of global environmental activists hear Almir Suruí's declaration of sacrifice? Though his plea appeared on a few websites, the response was negligible. Indeed, when I search the Internet for any indication Suruí has been heeded, I come up with nothing. To my horror, the invasion goes on—today it continues at a much greater scale under the orders of right-wing Brazilian President Jair Bolsonaro, a committed political enemy of indigenous people. There seems to be no one in Brazil's demonstrably corrupt and incompetent government to stop it. The genocide against the forest was the kind of injustice and aggression that had spurred me to action so long ago, inspired by the simple idea that Suruí had so succinctly expressed: my future is the same as yours.

APATHY

We are only gradually beginning to listen. We've been warned. Hurricanes, fires, floods, and extreme temperatures, like slingshots, have cracked the outer consciousness. But in most practical respects human life goes on unchanged amidst quickening deregulation and degradation, particularly in the United States, Brazil, and Indonesia. Some version of winter still comes, and the spring, and after that the summer and fall. There doesn't yet seem enough reason to act.

Too massive to comprehend, too distant in time and space, too dispersed in its nature: no wonder we can't quite face the eco-crisis. Yet isn't this the thinnest of fictions? Writing in 1955, Rachel Carson noted that warming caused by "widespread change of climate" was "now well recognized." One has the distinct feeling that Americans in general view the existence of global warming as white Americans view racism: hardly a problem at all. At heart, this is a failure of empathy, of seeing oneself in another. Should Almir Suruí's plea land in our in-box, it isn't very likely we would try to comprehend it. It certainly isn't likely we would stop purchasing diamonds or mahogany furniture or beef. The reason for this is empathy's near-opposite, apathy.

As a failure of political institutions, ecological crisis breeds apathy, born of the apparent sense that problems can't be solved, that nothing will ever change. As apathy gathers and settles in, it becomes brutal in its indifference to truth and reason, and contributes to paralysis. The thinnest of fictions needs the heaviest of heavies to enforce it. The bully given great power as a head of state has emerged as a real danger to planetary health in an age of apathy and fear, for he—it appears always to be a man—uses apathy to denigrate knowledge, normative evidence, and expertise. This sort of leader, whom we know as Putin, Trump, Bolsonaro, Erdogan, and Modi, among others, has emerged in our time as a force of eco-destruction.

The bully's great lie renders language impotent and truth irrelevant, which in turn stirs apathy, nurtures ambivalence, and produces dissonance. The lie goes something like this: *Show me global warming, I don't see it. Tell me precisely how you know that it causes more powerful storms. We've always had storms, and we've always had hot weather. How can you predict what will happen in twenty or fifty years? The weatherman can't even predict tomorrow's weather. If you want to speak about facts, then you should know the climate has always been changing. There was an ice age once and there's going to be another one in the future.* The liar distracts, veers off subject. *This global warming nonsense is made up by pin-headed liberals who want to tell me how to live. It's some kind of conspiracy to keep me from driving. It's a hoax, perpetrated by the Chinese!*

All this dissonance, like the hum of interference, won't allow us to think clearly. Just as we need to think clearly, examine evidence, and understand the fullest consequences, the bully casts doubt on the entire train of thought.

Experiencing this day after day, I'm reminded of painful bullying in my school years, in particular a ninth-grade Social Studies classroom, one day in 1983. I recall it here to illustrate the danger of illiberal fictions. The image that appears to me from that day is from the point of view of the left side of the classroom where I sat, surrounded by other kids' bodies and their heads, desks, and restless feet. But, as I meditate on this experience, a second view manifests in my mind's eye: I see the room from above, as if the rows of desks composed the columns of a temple from classical Greece, holding up the pediment of knowledge. The teacher stood at the head of the class, at the point of the pediment. We sat in five rather Doric columns extending to the back of the room. He wrote on the board: November 4, 1979. It was the end of the class period, throwaway time. He was in a generous mood. There was to be extra credit, he announced, for the student who knew what happened on that date. I did. It was the kind of thing I knew because I paid attention, because I was interested in politics and world affairs, because I absorbed the news. I raised my hand. I don't think it was long until the teacher called on me. "The Iran hostages were taken," I said, confidently but off-handedly. I liked to be off-handed. It was my only way, at fourteen, before discovering William O. Douglas and the concept of nature, to feel cool.

The teacher nodded in agreement. "Iranian revolutionaries took over the American embassy and took everyone hostage. He gets the extra credit." The teacher then turned sideways to face the board. As I was sitting in the second column halfway down, the teacher's back was now turned to me. He was thick, like a retired defensive lineman. In the fourth column, toward the base, someone raised his hand. A hard voice, like gum beaten between the jaws, and at the same time, smooth as ice, unsticky, detached. The voice and the eraser in the teacher's hand were the same. "He said it was when they rescued the hostages not when they took the hostages. Everybody heard. Now he's pretending he got it right." And then he laughed.

The student's name was Mike. He liked to fuck with people. He cheated on tests. With his back to me, the teacher faced Mike. They saw eye to eye. Now shut out, I groaned. "What? That isn't true. I know because it was November—." November—yes, dates stuck in my head, they had a form, an architecture.

The rescue was in January, at the same time Reagan was inaugurated. I knew that, and why. But facts no longer mattered.

"Ha-ha, he's trying to lie. He's lying. But we all know what he said." Mike, who had no curiosity about Social Studies or world affairs, no inclination to study, now seized the room. Most kids let themselves believe Mike. He used cruelty to make them laugh. "Look at him all red-faced 'cause he got caught." Now I hear it this way: *If you want to speak about facts, then you should know the climate has always been changing.*

"You're the one lying!" I shouted. I looked around, scared and defiant. Something was being taken away: the dignity that comes from speaking and being heard. The dignity of reason. The loss of the dignity of reason is another cause of our paralysis in the face of the ecological crisis. It produces self-doubt, and self-doubt confusion. "I said it! The hostages were taken in November—."

Shrugs up and down the rows of desks, like birds nestling into the flutes of the columns. There was no reason for anyone but me to be unambivalent. Why, anyway, if you couldn't stop laughing?

There was no way I could comprehend that reality—the truth as I knew it to exist—had terminally shifted. I didn't know what to do. Desperate now, I added more information, which only made me sound more pompous (whereas Mike had become the class's voice of reason), or as if I was trying to cover up a lie. "It couldn't have been when they were rescued. They were rescued in January, 1981." By the end of it my voice had faded. It had lost all power.

The liar's most dangerous tool is to delegitimize. To deny a lie made by a liar who insists you are the one lying is harder than telling a lie in the first place. The denial quickly becomes righteous, indignant, and uncomfortably shame-filled. You shouldn't have to deny it if you never did lie. As this happens the liar gains strength. His position, watching you squirm, solidifies. And his power becomes the only thing that matters, defying reason. (He also gets better and better at the lie with each successive claim.)

Once the first lie is made, the entire foundation of truth is broken. Anything can be believed. Aggression sustains the lie, that's the liar's secret. Truth, on the other hand, is fragile. Truth is complicated. Truth is difficult to pin down, exactly, and facts, as recordings of dynamic real life, can change. The liar understands implicitly how to exploit the difficulty in obtaining full clarity. It helps if the liar controls a powerful nation. It helps if the liar is a tool of a political party that itself is a tool of the oligarchical families who control the oil and gas industries, who have the most to gain if global warming opens the Arctic to drilling and the most to lose if mass action saves it from intractable harm. It helps if those industries are granted power to spread the lie. Finding an agreed truth is no longer a possibility. Dictatorial climate predators like Vladimir Putin, Bolsonaro, and Trump, and the broader voices in and beyond the petrochemical industry, profit from confusion. As with those who deny the Holocaust, confusion is their goal.

"All right, no extra credit," the teacher concluded. He erased the date from the board. The bell rang right into the commotion followed by a void—the floor of truth had after all caved in. After that I don't recall exactly how long my doubt and despair lingered. Tortured by bullying in those days, I would often lash out, lose my cool, make a fool of myself. I learned to sense how easily untruth can be used to distort and destroy. Today, as I write this, our head of state is Mike; each day he fucks with our known and shared reality. That power manifests as a tyranny of lies.

But lies are only one factor producing apathy. "Clichés, stock phrases, adherence to conventional, standardized codes of expression and conduct have the socially recognized function of protecting us against reality," wrote Hannah Arendt in her follow-up to "The Banality of Evil," a 1977 essay called "Thinking." How clearly she described the power of the climate predator. Stir those clichés and stock phrases into the general ambivalence and you'll erase the capacity for careful thought.

In the newer essay Arendt continued to struggle over Eichmann's evil acts. In her mind they emerged from something like apathy, not "stupidity but *thoughtlessness*" (emphasis in the original), and were then reflected in the acts of regular Germans. The absence of thought means the abandonment of the instinct to question what seems most troubling about human experience and the objective world around us, she wrote. The absence of thought demeans and devalues the act of thought, which in Arendt's formulation is the search for truth and the search for meaning, both.

This is not a definitive process, and it aches, no matter the subject of inquiry. The ecological crisis is singularly hard to discuss because of the implied guilt and the maudlin end: a steamy (and simultaneously desiccated) apocalypse. It requires that we first overcome doubt and then fix our minds for more than a minute and concentrate on the idea of extreme discontinuity: that, in fact, the world of our grandchildren will be defined foremost by misery and suffering, famine, drought, and war.

Scientists are already resigned to the mounting rate of change on Earth. Some of them are exploiting the opportunity to study previously inaccessible places like the Arctic and also to witness the profound biological transformation that's mostly invisible to the layperson. On top of this expanding exploration, scientists are discovering the existence of yet unknown beings, some who live in tiny areas of the biosphere. (Perhaps two or even six million species are unknown to man, according to E.O. Wilson). In this indeed blossoming research something notable is going on.

Following the lead of the pioneering biologist Lynn Margulis and environmental scientist M. Beth Dempster, researchers have begun to focus on collections of living organisms called holobionts, rather than examining single species in isolation. Because most beings on Earth are sympoietic and not autopoietic—that is, organized collectively, not as individuals—these scientists are driven to understand the way that creatures, in the words of Donna Haraway, "become-together."

And how they die together. Interconnectivity means that when one being goes extinct, it may cause a chain reaction, a process that until now scientists have poorly understood. "Extinction is not a single point, not a single event, but more like an extended edge or a widened ledge," Haraway wrote so evocatively in *Staying with the Trouble*.

> Extinction is a protracted slow death that unravels great tissues of ways of going on in the world for many species, including historically situated people.

Sensing the guilt and despair associated with ecological destruction, Haraway is keen to closely observe the loss—this is, in part, what it means to stay with the trouble. Whatever you do, don't change the subject!

Sympoiesis, and its opposite, unraveling, open up new ways of seeing. "If it is true that neither biology nor philosophy any longer supports the notion of independent organisms in environments, that is, interacting units plus contexts/rules, then sympoiesis is the name of the game in spades," she wrote. Responses to the ecological crisis must acknowledge and embrace the interconnectivity of beings. To Haraway, this is the great irony of our time: that the term "Anthropocene," with its implication that the earth belongs to that one species, would take hold just as a much more dynamic multi-being consciousness emerges. Sympoiesis is our chance, perhaps, to reconceive of life on Earth, by seeing ourselves among many, by stepping out of the automatic and into the polyphonic. This is what Almir Suruí's father taught him: listen to the forest, it will teach you how to live.

"Think we must; we must think!" wrote Haraway, adapting Hannah Arendt's observations of genocide to the ecological crisis. Perhaps crisis must be full-blown to bring enough clarity of thought—yet even so, not necessarily action. Crisis never allows time for reflection. (Reflection comes later, in a courtroom or tribunal.) Crisis overwhelms. Crisis replaces thinking with instinct, and instinct may be absent of thought. This is why we marvel at those who, in an emergency, remain clear-headed and calm and seem to know what to do.

My fear is that we will move directly from paralysis to frenzy. Neither allows for thought. The weakest will suffer the most.

DELUSIONS

More than seventy-five years later, the particular moral profile of Eichmann's crimes retains its power of intrigue, an eclipse of the human ideal from which it is impossible to look away. In the recent film *Operation Finale*, about Mossad's capture of Adolf Eichmann in Buenos Aires, where he was living incognito, director Chris Weitz personalized the tension between Eichmann and Mossad agent Peter Malkin. Frequently, the camera moves to a memory of a woman in a forest trying to hide her three children, one an infant, from swarming Nazi soldiers. The woman is Fruma, Malkin's sister. Later, as Malkin, who has captured Eichmann and brought him to a safe house for questioning, works over the impassive Eichmann, the Nazi asks, sensing a personal motivation, "Who did we take from you, Peter?"[15]

In another harrowing scene, the film imagines that Eichmann had ordered the capture of hundreds of Jews from a forest, including Fruma and her children. They've been forced to dig a massive trench—their grave. In the moment before the fatal order to murder the people now trapped in the trench, Fruma holds up her infant, Malkin's nephew, so that Eichmann can see him and choose whether to order the murder of a baby. This scene plays out in Eichmann's memory not as horror, but as triumph over mere sentiment, even as Fruma's brother stands before him and even as Eichmann has signaled, with his question, a false gesture of empathy. "Who did you lose?" In the fog of the winter forest, Eichmann notices Fruma and the child. He registers their existence. A moment later he gives the order to fire.

15. Eichmann is only able to imagine that an individual would act to revenge a personal injury and, in a transactional sense, balance the scales. He can't conceive of either the abstract public good or a specific societal motivation for justice. In these particular ways, Eichmann's ethos, such as it is, suggests Donald J. Trump.

We too have a gun pointing at us—a version of the same gun, of course. The U.N. estimates that humans have a single decade to radically reduce carbon emissions to avoid catastrophe. Under that gun, my instinct is the same as Fruma's: to hold up the not-yet-born but not unlikely child, who I imagine will one day stir this future grandfather's heart, so that all of us can see what we're doing. In that collective sense, we are Eichmann's men, taking aim at the child, and we are Fruma both. There is little indication that we can bear to look and none, so far as I know, that we will be able to stop events from unfolding. Remarkably, we haven't fired yet, or at least the bullets haven't been universally fatal. There must still be time.

I don't think we demean the Holocaust by comparing it to what will come, the genocide of Earth life by the richest and most powerful earthlings. In 2040, twenty years from now, my grandchild, I calculate, will be five. In Philadelphia, where I live, there will be thirty-five days a year with a high temperature of ninety degrees Fahrenheit or more (there were twelve when I was born). This is the kind of heat we can expect at the start of the crisis. The number of days of extreme heat will continue to rise through the twenty-first century and could reach sixty or more by 2100.

Heat is particularly dangerous in a city with high humidity. When the humidity is one hundred percent and the temperature ninety, it becomes nearly impossible to function. By 2040, sea levels will likely rise by two feet at least. Because of the flooding that spills forward from rising seas, my neighborhood, six blocks from the river, may be lost. Farther afield, Earth's coral reefs will near complete and permanent bleaching. Desertification may cause the entire Middle East to be uninhabitable. Rising acid in the oceans will destroy the basis of marine life—phytoplankton, krill, and zooplankton—unleashing an unstoppable spiral of death. I hold the baby up, an invisible, imagined baby, in desperation. Look! The hope and possibility of an infant child.

Normal people can act without thought but also with determined courage and care. Which is human instinct? It may be that humans will act to protect other humans over other beings—over nature, certainly, as that is the foundation of modernity. But it could also be likely that we distinguish among humans and decide who is worth protecting and who ought to be discarded. (We might remind ourselves that Eichmann, as one who perpetrated such a choice, was himself once an infant, filled with possibility, no different from the infants he condemned to death.) That I am worth saving and you are not—according to arbitrary classifications of skin color or national origin, religion or wealth—is perhaps the most enduring moral delusion of human history. And as ideology the most dangerous, for it promises absolution from moral choice, thinking, and even the practice of compassion.

Let's posit (a bit fancifully) for a moment that in our age such value distinctions are becoming more and more rare and that most of us agree to believe in the essential equality of each human being. Then let's look around at the extraordinary inequalities within and among societies and think about them: How did they come about? It seems to me there are two conclusions one might draw from this observation. The first demands further investigation into the systems, such as capitalism and colonialism, that have created the inequalities, to understand more precisely how they came about. This conclusion suggests that choices were made, and not by accident, and that history isn't inevitable. Outcomes are the accumulation of moral choices and political actions. In this manner, the future is also open to choice and action. The second conclusion, after the same normative evaluation, avers that this is the way things are, and, in a kind of circular logic, that people aren't inherently equal after all and will never be. Some five to seven million years of history prove it.

I composed this little thought diversion in order to consider the work of a British ecologist, Chris D. Thomas, on the success and failure of plant and animal species. Thomas is an enthusiastic field researcher and lover of nature and the kind of person we depend on to think for us and to direct our actions in a time of peril. In a recent book, *Inheritors of the Earth*, Thomas asks a version of the question I have asked: What's to explain the relative success or failure—not among unequal human societies but between humans and other plant and animal species? He draws his reader to conclusion two, that the process of success for some and failure for others is inevitable. Here's what Thomas says of the present upheaval of Earth. Note his strikingly dispassionate, nearly bloodless, voice and its disregard for the impact of human moral choice and political action: "Whatever period we are considering, species have moved to take advantage of new opportunities that have arisen from time to time, just as they died out in places where conditions become unsuitable. It is the way our biological planet works. It is the same again today."

Thomas is ambivalent about efforts, commonly supported by ecologists, to protect native species from the invasion of foreign ones in order to conserve an imagined order. (To his intellectual credit, Thomas is not a believer in purity as a political or ecological concept.) There are only natives to Earth in his construct (indeed no one is better than the other); the most adaptable adapt. And adaptation is a kind of eternal, immutable force; it goes on without moral judgment or choice. In place of a backwards gaze to a more perfect past, Thomas suggests instead that we ought to celebrate "new biological successes." He writes with knowledge and enthusiasm and even empathy for the lost but with a kind of gleeful eye to evolution: "A world without change is not an available option."

I'd like to accept this new positivism as insurance against despair. As we imagine loosening the paralysis, we will have to commit ourselves to stop fearing change. Thomas points out, as do many other biologists and geologists, that mass extinction events seem horrifying but ultimately make way for a new bout of life. The evolution of cyanobacteria in the Proterozoic eon more than two billion years ago brought forth toxic oxygen that destroyed most of life on Earth. But creatures that could metabolize oxygen developed in their place and caused an explosion of life forms. We don't remember or particularly care about those that were wiped out.

For the time being, I'll accept Thomas's thinking. If the current extinction, produced by man, is the sixth, then can't we imagine a seventh, eighth, ninth, or tenth? Imagining such scenarios is the work of another theorist, Dorion Sagan, son of biologist Lynn Margulis (inventor of the concept of sympoiesis) and Carl Sagan. "Life is an energy-transducing phenomenon," Dorion Sagan wrote in an essay ("Terra in the Cyanocene," in *Arts of Living on a Damaged Planet*), notably without mentioning specific species or even familiar life forms. From an even further distance than Chris Thomas, Sagan observes the way tiny organisms have accessed and stored energy and recycled waste efficiently, "keeping the energy expenditure game going" for nearly four billion years. Life forms of "fabulous complexity"—of, in one of Sagan's examples, "forams and diatoms and dinoflagellates"—are quite adept at efficient energy exchange, and will never, ultimately, give up (until the earth itself is extinguished by some internal or external force).

Multi-species collaborations, such as in Almir Suruí's forest, or at least the forest of Almir's father before loggers and miners wrecked the balance, carry out this same process at mammal and avian and reptile scale. Human monocultures of cities and farms are the least capable of using and recycling energy; they threaten to end the energy expenditure game, and thus life as we know it, prematurely. This threat—humanity's danger to life on the planet—is a cause of "worry, but not despair," Sagan wrote. Life on Earth pours back in ever-more-fervid form with each subsequent extinction.

By radically increasing the timescale of analysis, Sagan and Thomas present us with a way to avoid moral responsibility for ransacking life on Earth. This comes, to me at least, as a reprieve; like a gaze into the impossibility of the cosmos, this shift fundamentally ruptures my sense of self. No longer do I feel so bloated with power and puffed with responsibility; for a moment, at least, the entire notion of this book, a search for a moral response to eco-crisis, feels impossibly overblown and rather silly.

But as I read further in Thomas's book, contemplating the chemical accident that produced oxygen and the capacity of certain organisms to make use of the oxygen, I come across this: "Crickets, crabs, cuttlefish, cod, caiman, crows and cheetahs would not be possible but for that oxygen." The sentence surprised me not because of the alliteration per se, but because of what I sense it means, why it would have occurred to the biologist to compose it. Thomas may not work within a philosophical framework of moral choice and action, but he is sentimental. He conceived of a "c" list to associate various animals that we humans serenade in song, evoke in poetry, and admire on film in order to make the distant chemical process feel real. To make it meaningful he had to show the reader why it might matter: we feel for those critters, they're part of the mesh. We don't care to lose them even as we chase them to extinction.

My point (and perhaps his) is that we aren't bloodless killers like cyanobacteria; we may be craven, carnivorous, cloying, yes, but we are also courageous, concerned, caring, and conscientious, and this, our essential contradiction, is the cause of our crisis (and another element of paralysis). We can't, and shouldn't, keep our distance from the life and death inside and outside of us. Distant observers we are not. A newborn Paiter Suruí child is prohibited from eating corn, chicken, and armadillo, and until one year old is denied scaleless fish, monkey, wild boar, and tapir. Managing harm for a child or a family, a society or an ecosystem, is also a human instinct. For this reason, for example, Almir Suruí's ancestors took only exactly the amount of game, fruit, and honey they needed from the forest; they rotated crops so as to not deplete the soil, and they rotated jobs within the community to reinforce the concept of balance in life.

In every culture, human beings are elaborately tied to other creatures. "Look at this *mokaï* shrub with its round, bright green leaves," Almir Suruí's father told him. "If you rub these leaves on your arm, its spirit will protect you and make you stronger for carrying wood." Connection to the external world begins with touch and feeling. By virtue of intimacy, practice, observation, and myth, these relationships have developed over millennia across all cultures. As flawed as we are, we relate to the world on these deeply wrought grounds that are themselves reflections of history, identity, language, and religion. We are, in fact and glory, sentimental beings. As anarchist and feminist Voltairine de Cleyre wrote: "There is feeling in the world, and a very great quantity of it." Why else prosecute Adolf Eichmann? Perhaps for pride, in the case of the Jewish people and the infant state of Israel, or a sense of redemption, which is something like justice. In the case of the ecological crisis, we inject shame, for in murdering Earth aren't we murdering ourselves? Isn't our survival co-dependent on other life forms? Sympoiesis says it is.

But rapidly developing technologies in robotics, artificial intelligence, food processing, and manipulation of DNA suggest that we modernists are ever-becoming the masters of life and not life's contingency. The brother of a close friend is a Smithsonian scientist who studies forest biomass. He suggests that if we were to attempt to restrict ourselves and our human potential for the sake of protecting nature, we would act in denial of evolution, which commands us to preserve our species. As ecological systems collapse, how will we as a species respond? He says we are hard-wired to choose to protect human life over all else:

morally, for the sake of survival, this is the choice we must make. If we wish to prolong and sustain life, it must be human life, he says. Just as a mother protects her babies, in the great unraveling of life on Earth, instinct will require extreme anthropocentrism.

As I see it, though, war is most certainly what will result if we try to protect human life over all else. A desire will emerge to save one kind of human and not the other, and the choices that result will be made along the predictable lines of race, class, religion, and tribe. It won't be pretty. A combination of war and ecological destruction (two elements that feed each other in a ferocious cycle) will produce, in the lifetime of my grandchild, a desolate dystopian landscape. The unborn innocent grandchildren of the world are not equal, and their inequality will be exposed when tides swallow cities and deserts devour abundant rivers. We will choose sides, and some will decide, on seeing the human genocide, to protect what's left of nature. Fighting among the rich will divert attention from the poor, it doesn't take much imagination to predict, as certain people will try to stake claim to the highest ground or the richest fields of energy. The war of all wars will be over the Arctic.

However, I can see a second, perhaps overlapping future that might emerge should we protect human lives over and above all others, should we refuse to accept the breadth and depth of interdependence. This vision is of a sleek interior world, shut off from all nonhuman species but microorganisms (and those kept at bay), with every other element but our own flesh and blood (and perhaps that too) manufactured. It looks perhaps like some version of science fiction, but, in reality, versions already exist. A day of travel by air probably goes something like this: subway, through an underground tunnel, to airport; mechanical conveyance into airport and into a singularly sealed-off human world (aside from the occasional boxed pet or emotional support animal); onto airplane. Depending on the number of connections and the particular kind of transport that awaits on the other side, one may avoid sensory contact with any other sort of living being (aside from invisible ones), as well as soil of any kind, bud, wind, and rain. After hours and hours, the traveler feels ransacked by the extreme and unwavering detachment—or perhaps, just the same, ecstatic upon release at the first kiss of humidity, scent of fragrant blossom, ruffle of leaves.

It isn't difficult to extrapolate from this present experience to a near future of scorching heat and complete detachment. Should we begin to live predominantly inside (as indeed quarantine during the coronavirus pandemic taught us to do), we'll have to fill that world with semblant nature and semblant food. This sounds to me distinctly dystopian, but perhaps I am mistaken to think that life, under these circumstances, would somehow count for less. Is it less human to ski a manufactured mountain inside a shopping mall? Are the snow crystals sprayed on the invented mountain less real? They form when water hits a certain temperature. Does the air rushing across your face as you fly down the trail feel any different than it would on Mont Blanc on a February day? Brilliant engineers can make conditioned air feel like anything they want—like a memory, for example, of an alpine afternoon in winter. Is it likewise less authentic to swim under an engineered waterfall than a real one in a Central American rainforest? The water, too, can be finely tuned to startle, to elicit screams of joy, to zoom the heart. Art fabricators can digitally recreate a mural by Giotto, with its images of humble people amidst divine clouds and donkeys, stark cliffs and trees, and rivers of sky offering an opening to divinity, and perhaps you would never know the difference. In front of the original, do you feel the artist's bravura hand present, do you find yourself moved to think that seven hundred years ago Giotto and his apprentices, humans as you, stood on this floor and conjured the angels? Perhaps that never occurs to you. Should someone build a recreation of the Cappella degli Scrovegni and install fabricated versions of Giotto's murals, would you feel any less moved? Possibly the answer depends on knowing. Should you have no idea the chapel you're standing in is a fake and the murals generated by a machine, you might succumb to the sheer intensity of vision, perhaps as you might under the torrent of a man-made waterfall in a counterfeit grotto. Should you know, on the other hand, that the chapel is a fake, you may become distracted by the art of the fakery. Just that tiny distraction could separate you enough from the art to render it powerless in the way it was intended (it may contain a new power—to demonstrate man's capacity for fakery). This same separation threatens our relationship to nature.

Yet pretension can become its own reality, authenticity a matter of perspective. We pretend we are who we aren't and sometime later we become that pretended person. As a child I pretended our post-War suburban house was something like the kind of stone farmstead typical of Bucks County, Pennsylvania, where I grew up. This same instinct contributed to my father's interest in realism, in antique paintings of rural scenes. He and my mother purchased vivid oils framed with primitive pine boards, as if to say we, too, were part of an iconography of country life. My father and I built a patio meant to extend the pretense and surrounded it with native plantings. The remnants of a hardwood forest served as the backdrop to the garden, and sitting in it one might squint and imagine the rolling hills weren't embroidered with suburban developments, wide asphalt streets, and lawns maintained with nitrogen and Roundup. In reality, the soaring trees provided protection for significant forest biomass, yet in a chimerical form—covering only a dozen acres.

The sliver of forest, however, in its constant presence in my life as a child, made me aware of larger nearby forests. Though themselves constrained and compromised, they invited something inside me to blossom, a symbiosis of spirit that awakens fully in the forest or meadow or naked in the stream. Without this contact I am not fully myself.

When the twentieth-century suburbanite (like an eighteenth-century English gentleman or Marie Antoinette in her shepherdess hut) constructed a simulacrum of nature to live in, despite being pretense or playacting, it offered an invitation and opportunity to be drawn into the real thing, to develop a truer relationship with and understanding of nature. But if all that is left to us is a digital recreation, we lose the opportunity. Pretending is thus a window to our earthly nature that will be shut by the ecological crisis, if all we are left with is the fake. Should we be overwhelmed by the intensity of the crisis, we are likely to work harder to master nature or eliminate it, fracturing our measured relationship to nature—which for most people isn't uniformly intimate or distant but exists on a sliding scale, a matter of degrees.

We live in the sliding scale. For this reason, I wonder if Timothy Morton's mesh isn't itself a bit of a delusion. Morton believes, if I understand him right, that the problem of the ecological crisis is ultimately a manifestation of distance between humans and nature fostered originally by the domestication of plants and animals through agriculture. Accepting the mesh, in Morton's narrative, will eventuate a paradigm shift away from mastery and control. This sounds ideal, but my own experience in the lakeside garden suggests that we don't want the mesh any more than we want to live inside all the time. Neither our brains nor our bodies will give up some sense of control (developing for 14,000 years, agriculturalism is deeply embedded in our lifeways and instincts). Control is a hammer of a word that includes assessment, determination, judgment, desire, and responsibility. Control is the care of a small farmer tending to her fields and animals. It sits on the moral ground from which we assess our surroundings, confer them value, and ultimately, come to believe in love and justice.

I was reminded of this broad range of negotiation with nature during a recent hike in the Rocky Mountains with my carefully observing friend, Harmon. We started at a Rocky Mountain National Park trailhead near Eldora, Colorado, and headed to Caribou Lake, two hours up the trail. We arrived at the trailhead at seven on an August morning, the air and ground frosty. The parking lot was already full; Harmon explained to me that people who live in Boulder love to hike—it defines who they are. They get up early, put on fancy gear, and drive their 4×4 vehicles an hour up a rutted road and then spend the day in wilderness. There's nothing strange about this. Only it tells us—at the upper end of both the income scale and the scale of nature immersion—the degrees to which people connect themselves to nature. Vehicles account for one-fifth of American carbon dioxide emissions; they are also about the only mode of access to the wilderness. People drive, park, hike, and fish, as Harmon did while I watched, and then they return to Boulder for an afternoon beer. Around noon, when we came off the trail, the parking lot was overwhelmed, and a traffic jam, at the mouth of the backcountry, held us up for twenty minutes.

When he was a young boy, William O. Douglas was stricken with polio and left with spindly legs. The Yakima foothills and the distant Cascades lured him to strength as tantalizing possibility; he most often went alone, leaving home on foot, returning days later from the far ridge. He never, certainly, got a ride. One evening as a boy, he walked a trail and listened as the Chinook wind blew from the distant rim, reached the sage at his feet and his cheek moments later. The Chinook, he wrote, "ran its fingers through my hair and rippled away in the darkness. It was a friendly wind, friendly to man throughout time."

> It became for me that night a measure of the kindliness of the universe to man, a token of the hospitality that awaits man when he puts foot on this earth. It became for me a promise of the fullness of life to him who, instead of shaking his fist at the sky, looks to it for health and strength and courage.

Our trip to Caribou Lake was meant to resemble this experience, to get enough of it for our own health and strength and courage, from the joy of the high mountain views, the bright air and open meadows. For this same reason I sit at my desk and listen to the hundreds of birds who live in the street trees and the rusted cornices of the buildings on the block. The wind stirring the branches carries the brine of the river and the

Atlantic Ocean beyond: these degrees of nature are tokens, indeed, and for me they often suffice until I can access a bit of wilderness.

In its hospitality, Earth invites us out of our skin— out in mind, out in time, out in scale. It invites us to feel love. This feeling is a Romantic surge, but I don't think that it is delusion. William O. Douglas could touch the wind from his high mountain perch, and the wind taught him how to be human. The pain of losing this generous touch has caused me to attempt this book. The despair I feel day by day is the despair of that loss: what I was given as an earthling—the promise of the fullness of life—by my own actions I am taking away.

RESPONSIBILITY

While I was drafting the original version of this book, a right-wing federal circuit judge, Brett Kavanaugh, was confirmed as an associate justice of the Supreme Court. Very possibly, his appointment, which solidi-fied a conservative majority on the Court, will allow oil and gas oligarchs and their allies to successfully challenge the regulatory foundation of America's en-vironmental laws, including those meant to reduce emissions of carbon dioxide and methane. If we ulti-mately are unable to stop events from unfolding, the Supreme Court's extreme ideological imbalance may be significantly to blame.

With the vote on Kavanaugh's nomination near-ing, several women came forward to accuse him of sexual assault and sexual impropriety as a young man. They inspired a protest movement that nearly derailed the nomination. The resistance came to a peak outside an elevator in the Russell Senate Office Building, where two activists confronted a Republican senator from Arizona, Jeff Flake, who was seen as open to the argument that Kavanaugh was unfit for the Court but unlikely to vote against the nomination. The two women, Maria Gallagher and Ana Maria Archila, were furious that the senator would ignore the highly credible testimony of the one accuser allowed to speak to the Senate, Christine Blasey Ford. Flake stood motionless, looking toward the ground as Gallagher told him that voting for Kavanaugh would signal to survivors of sexual assault that their pain didn't matter. "Look at me when I'm talking to you," she demanded. When Flake said nothing in response, Archila asked, "Do you think that Brett Kavanaugh is telling the truth? Do you think that he's able to hold the pain of this country and repair it? That is the work of justice."

The way that justice works is you recognize harm, you take responsibility for it, and then you begin to repair it.

I perceived Archila's words like a hard and unexpected swallow. No air passed through the national dialog in that moment, and then a rush of it came; the women's courage was like a warm and strengthening wind. When I watched the confrontation on an Internet video, I took note of Archila's distinctive south-western accent, betraying the confluence of Mexican, American and indigenous language and culture. I stopped the video, rewound it slightly, and played the last part over and over. "The way that justice works . . ." I was astonished to hear an American citizen speak to a U.S. senator about reconciliation, a concept of justice Americans have rarely acknowledged. The way justice works in the U.S. has never been about societal healing and repair—otherwise, reparations would have long since been paid to Native Americans and African Americans. The only attempt, post–Civil War, aptly named Reconstruction, very quickly produced a new wave of disunity and violence rather than unity and healing. Justice in this country isn't a restorative communal experience, the many above the one. It has instead primarily been a tool to protect individual liberty. Archila's concept, it was plain in her voice, emerged from experience with colonizers and perhaps with genocide and dictatorship, situations that have empowered tribunals to speak broadly for the good of the people, to heal the wounds of the oppressed and the oppressors.[16] This is the kind of justice to apply to the ecological crisis, a work of healing to give back to the exploited—humans and other creatures alike—that which makes them alive. Restorative justice works

16. In *The Fire Next Time* and other writings James Baldwin taught us that hatred and injustice cause considerable dehumanizing pain to the aggressor as well as the victim.

for the many and not the few on the basis that both victim and perpetrator can be healed jointly.

I began this work on the eve of Yom Kippur, for Jews the annual moment of taking account, recognizing the harm in ourselves. It has brought me to the instinct to repair, which Jews call *tikkun olam*, literally to heal the world. *Tikkun olam* took on new urgency after the Holocaust and since then has given Jews a powerful framework for seeking justice.

Some years ago, traveling in the Middle East, I took a photograph of a graffiti wall in the Tel Aviv neighborhood Florentin, which I've kept as the background image on my computer. The neighborhood is near Alma Beach, where Israeli Jews and Israeli and Palestinian Muslims swim side by side. At the center of my photograph is a wheat-paste drawing of two Earth-shaped heads with human features; one has taken the other in its arms and a Band-Aid holds them together. Though it is likely a vision of Arab-Israeli peace, I've always interpreted the image as an allegory for human beings—separate from but intimate with nature—healing the earth. This is the urge of *tikkun olam*.

Raising the prospective grandchild to the eyes of the world, and to the air and the trees and the stars, can we recognize the harm we've already caused and the injury to come? Are any of us willing to first imagine and then repair the future? Or, one year from now, or five, must we remain bathed in thoughtlessness? Paralyzed by the distance between the need to act and the impossibility of action, we will have perpetrated a horrifying trick on ourselves: the denial of the possibility of a future.

In the Holocaust, the landscape of the coming anti-future was pre-imagined. We can find it in Primo Levi's description of Auschwitz, "desperately and essentially opaque and gray."

> This huge tangle of iron, concrete, mud, and smoke is the negation of beauty. Its roads and buildings have been given names like ours, numbers or letters, or inhuman and sinister ones. Within its precincts not a blade of grass grows, the soil is impregnated with the poisonous juices of coal and petroleum, and nothing is alive but machines and slaves—and the former are more alive than the latter.

The negation of nature as the essence of the anti-future is, as Levi discovered, the negation of hope. For nature produces hope and hope draws us closer to healing. The prospect of healing is the impetus for justice. And this is why we must find a way to act now: we need nature to lead us to healing. In a world full of feeling, the desire for justice grows paramount. Recognize the harm, take responsibility for it, and begin to repair it. This is the kind of thinking that must—yes, it must—shake us loose. In a decade it will be too late to avert the crisis in its incomprehensible magnitude because of the cumulative effect of our thoughtless emissions. In two decades, it will be too late because the extent of the poison in the system will overwhelm even nature's own inexorable capacity to transform. All systems will collapse.

Amidst the sinister sickness of Auschwitz every instant might have felt too late. Yet Levi recalls in vivid detail a single day in late winter 1944 when he began to anticipate the hope of spring and contemplate the possibility of justice. At noon the prisoners in Levi's barrack became aware of a fifty-liter vat of soup that one of them, Templer, had secreted away. The soup was rancid. The Polish workers it was meant for had refused to eat it. There is no pride in hope or hunger. Each man in the barrack got three liters of soup to add to the usual meager ration and a few turnips pilfered from an unguarded delivery truck. They devoured the spoiled soup with the savagery of animals, Levi noted. Something had awakened in them.

"Today," he wrote, "for the first time the sun rose bright and clear from the horizon of mud."

> For the first time we notice that on both sides of the road, even here, the meadows are green, because, without the sun, a meadow is as if it were not green.

The illuminated meadow spoke the volumes of the ages. It is speaking now. My grandchild will want to walk in that meadow. My god, I hope this desire remains—and not only the desire but also the possibility.

When I set out into a meadow and brush against the knife-edged grass and the needles and the thorns that puncture the skin and I breathe in the pepper and onion and mint and extend my awareness to the dragonfly and the hummingbird clearwing moth and to the hot tips of my own fingers in the air, I gain the distinct sense that all of this is enough. Here is pleasure and desire, weight and lightheadedness, and time—all of it concentrated around me. It's all sufficient. A meadow, like an imagined child, has some incalculable incipient force to mesmerize and to tantalize. What is life without such earthly gifts? When we lose these gifts, we lose what gives us hope; we lose the capacity and desire to overcome apathy, to undo paralysis. For we don't live only in the moment. Like Primo Levi we live toward something. If that something is a dark horror how will we stand to go on?

I am not a commodity

> The question that now begins to gnaw at your mind is more anguished: outside Penthesilea does an outside exist?
>
> Italo Calvino, *Invisible Cities*

MELANCHOLY

In what manner will we—again the plural pronoun—respond to dark horror? Or you, my imagined grandchild? I mean to ask how we might change our minds to avoid total ruin. Specific factors that collide with dynamic violence today—the overwhelming demand for return on capital, the sweeping reliance on global trade, and the intensification of agriculture—produced a sequence of climate change just over seven centuries ago. These modes of collective human behavior transformed a bacterial infection, *Yersinia pestis*, which kills black rats (the kind that live in close proximity to humans), into an epidemic killer of some fifty million people. For seven years beginning in 1346, rat fleas spread *Yersinia pestis*, bubonic plague, from dead rat to humans and on ships from humans to other humans and then to new populations of rats and back to humans newly crowded in cities and agricultural villages from Scandinavia to North Africa and the Middle East. The fleas leveled about 60 percent of the European population.

A team of Harvard University and University of Maine toxicologists, climate scientists, historians, and archeologists have documented, at least preliminarily, the extent to which the decimation of the people of Europe had a salutary effect on the environment, much as the collapse of global economic activity caused by the COVID-19 pandemic temporarily slashed the amount of measurable carbon dioxide and other gases and particulate matter in the atmosphere. As the withered population stopped smelting lead, lead pollution declined precipitously, the only time this has happened in the last 2,000 years.[17]

A century and a half after the epidemic petered out, Europeans, itchy with renewed ambition, sought new sources of wealth and power in the Americas. The European conquest of the indigenous peo-

17. "Next-generation Ice Core Technology Reveals True Minimum Natural Levels of Lead (Pb) in the Atmosphere: Insights from the Black Death." Alexander F. More, Nicole E. Spaulding, Pascal Bohleber, Michael J. Handley, Helene Hoffmann, Elena V. Korotkikh, Andrei V. Kurbatov, Christopher P. Loveluck, Sharon B. Sneed, Michael McCormick, and Paul A. Mayewski, *GeoHealth*, Volume 1, Issue 4, 31 May 2017, pp. 211–219.

ples of the Americas took much of the next century, and it resulted in the erasure of another fifty-five million people from Earth, victims of infectious diseases for which they had no immunity. A recent study by geographers at University College London tracks the cycles of carbon emission and carbon sequestration in the late fifteenth and early sixteenth centuries, arguing with clear evidence that the genocide of the fifty-five million indigenous people resulted in "human-driven global impact on the Earth System."[18]

As forests reclaimed land that had been used for agriculture by indigenous people, carbon in the atmosphere plummeted, and so did global temperatures. Freed of agriculture, forests the size of France regenerated in the Americas, absorbing carbon dioxide and cooling the planet substantially. We call the period that followed both episodes of human depopulation, from the early fourteenth century to the mid-nineteenth, the "Little Ice Age."[19]

Leaving aside the genocide that resulted from European conquest of the Americas—that we have no other term for that part of the world is a mark of the totality of the act—and leaving aside the reflowering of Europe it funded, the Renaissance following so-called

18. "Earth System Impacts of the European Arrival and Great Dying in the Americas after 1492." Alexander Koch, Chris Brierley, Mark M. Maslin, and Simon L. Lewis. *Quaternary Science Reviews*, Volume 207, 1 March 2019, pp. 13–36.

19. The two studies I've cited here offer new insight into the human impact on climate and the environment.

Dark Ages, let's return for a moment to the days of rapid societal change occurring before the rat fleas became infected. Quite a bit differently from what my generation was taught, the Dark Ages, or what we might simply call the turn of the second millennium, included periods of rapid social change, globalization, and urbanization. To a newly significant degree in this period, investment capital began to matter: Money had to produce money. A goat had to produce milk that could be exchanged for grain. And all around you, if you resided along the Silk Road or near the Mediterranean Sea, were traders, people who looked and sounded different, who followed some other religious rules, who saw their own possibility and power in the doing of business. No one knew it might produce plague. Clear more forest, those goats are valuable.

Glory to God, all of a sudden, the streets of places you'd never heard of were paved with gold! And what of it, you Genoan or Malagan or Tunisian or Samarkandian, you just needed to keep up and avoid getting your head chopped off. Be mobile and don't expect today to be just like yesterday or tomorrow like today. Let the poets and priests absorb the fractures in society; let them notice the ground rapidly shifting beneath the feet.

So you went along in the early second millennium—and so we go about doing our business today. Our business is to turn money into more money, and we do it chiefly by extracting Earth materials and smothering Earth systems—easily and quickly with the machinery of our invention. We call this mastery. Mastery is the highest human achievement. When we imagine ourselves humanists we seek to recognize and celebrate that achievement. We celebrate the highest excellence in science and art. We praise genius. When we praise others without celebrating ourselves, when we love one another and come to the aid of the less fortunate, we act humanely. To act humanely means to master aggression toward another human, subdue it. Only sometimes we slip up and subjugate others, we demonstrate man's inhumanity to man. This is an error, we tell ourselves. It can't be natural, or normal, or human, if humans are capable of such achievement and such loving kindness.

Unless, that is, the subjugation is directed at Earth, in which case it isn't called inhumanity, but the opposite: mastery. Resource extraction and processing (which produce 50 percent of global greenhouse gas emissions), industrial agriculture, and engineering for energy and transportation demand the highest level of human expertise, mastery of physics, time, and material. The high agricultural yields needed to feed eight billion humans demand highly engineered chemical fertilizers, and the cost to Earth is of no consequence in the calculations—most engineering and economic models don't attempt to account for it. To be a humanist, it turns out one must put human needs above all. The same is true for the effort to rapidly expand cities into sensitive wetlands, tidal basins, and coastline: purely quantitative analysis—with an eye toward profit and, perhaps, some social good, like housing—is the only consideration, particularly where, as in most of the world, regulatory mechanisms are weak. Greed is thus not the only problem. Favoring humans above all is. This celebrated and much lauded mastery requires poison and ecosystem destruction at what is, without exaggeration, an epic scale.

In this sense destruction of Earth sold as human mastery is expected—is required. For this reason, we don't seem to be able to stop blasting, drilling, and spraying—and with ever increasing masterful efficiency. Mastery, leading so often to the desire for and achievement of efficiency above all, creates a smoothness to human predation of Earth; technology allows us to exploit the planet's resources with calibrated ease. The calibrated smoothness is the end in itself. This is why we marvel at the genius of engineering. As a high achievement of modernity, it separates our hands from the dirty work. The mesmerizing machine becomes the end in itself. We focus on its quantitative achievements of scale, speed, and accuracy and lose track of what the machine is actually doing to Earth. This is the terror of mastery: a globe encased in concrete.

Writing in the early 1970s in the exquisite *Invisible Cities*,[20] Italo Calvino represented the eternally grinding engine as endless urban sprawl, one undistinguished city form running into the other, obliterating

20. In the English translation by William Weaver.

the landscape with "vague" buildings. The imagined apotheosis is Penthesilea, a "continuous city" so undefined that it appears to the resident or visitor "only the outskirts of itself." To experience such a formless city, as I'm reminded each time I cross the Delaware River and find myself driving on the long commercial highways of South Jersey, is to be—precisely—dehumanized. Going along, one overscaled intersection after the other, I feel my power, spontaneity, and desire draining out, the blood pooling at this traffic light and then that one and the next, the very opposite of the freedom I felt as a teenager behind the wheel for the first time. Bloodless: this is the feeling the perfect machine produces, of killing something already substantially dead. It is, in fact, numbing and mindless and depleting; the ache that it produces is the weight of melancholy—and this is well before total catastrophe has happened.

To get from A to B in this country, on this earth, we humans have become forced to use a car (in many places there is no other way). Eighty-eight million of them were sold worldwide in 2017—a hyperobject of metal, plastic, and grease. We humans have built our lives around them, to the point of social, personal, and ecological stress and exhaustion, trapping our bodies into a spatial prison, a prison as inviolable and as frighteningly surreal as the landscape of Penthesilea, while some of us profit from our total dependence. Imagine that as ambient beings on Earth we humans must pay to use a poisonous commodity in order to go about our lives and that the payment goes not to some collective that manages and regulates the adverse impacts of the poison but instead to multinational corporate conglomerates and filthy-rich oligarchs who profit while the rest of us become stressed out.

Once the black rats started to die in the middle of the fourteenth century, it took several weeks for the rat fleas to nibble a little *Yersinia pestis* and plant a deadly kiss. As the epidemic spread from Sicily in 1347 to booming Tunis in 1348 and to Algiers and Tangier and then to Sevilla and Cordoba in 1349, it left towns and cities in ruins, according to the historian Robert Irwin, and nothing, it seemed, could stop it, no wisdom or forbearance, no acts of prayer. To Muslim eyes, particularly, the ruins came to represent "monarchical injustice," writes Irwin in *Ibn Khaldun*, evidence of man's corruption and incompetent government. Here was failure written on the landscape and not only failure, but horrifying loss of all that was assumed to comprise the world, including fathers and sons, mothers and daughters, friends and foes. The impossibility of this loss became the source of extreme melancholy for both Muslims and Christians, a muted humbling, an ache for what was and what can't be. There wasn't much to do but wait for the End Times.

Driving recently in central Florida, where four- and five- and six- and seven-lane roads go on in eternal Penthesilean horror, one indistinguishable from the next, a Walgreens at every third intersection and the space between them chained with new car dealerships, auto garages, oil change and lube franchises, body shops, and gas stations—"pale buildings back-to-back in mangy fields," as Calvino precisely imagined it—I had the distinct feeling that the End Times had finally come. With each subsequent traffic light, the glare dull yet somehow piercing, the haze immobilizing, I grew more and more weary. Sedans, pickups, and SUVs bloated my vision in all directions. I crept along in a plastic and metal machine across the snuffed-out ground, and was it ground still, slicked with petrol and crushed gravel? Yes, only somehow inside out.

For a while I cursed at those who had done this to us, who had sacrificed *la tierra florida* for Florida. Then, recognition emerged as a kind of salvation: melancholy was a matter of mind, a mechanism of survival, this act of refusing hope. Florida produces melancholy because it might be *florida* or, more precisely, *florida* is still there, somewhere, in blotches of Spanish oaks and sweeps of marsh and the perfuming heat itself. Melancholy is produced by beauty that can't be manifest; it fundamentally quiets human ambition. Manifest as ache, in speech, song, art, and poetry, it absolves us of the need for mastery, for pessimism doubts the virtue of agency. Melancholy then appears to be a sensible response during ecological crisis. When each of us is responsible for the spiraling consequences of actions produced collectively across vast time and space—an impossible fate for an individual moral being—perhaps it is best to reject the instinct to act and fix and instead accede to lamentation.

When we destroy ourselves by any means, known or unknown, visible like war, or invisible like *Yersinia pestis*, we seek explanations beyond ourselves. We may even imagine, like some chroniclers of the plague, that destruction is inevitable. "The voice of existence in the world had called out for oblivion and restriction, and the world responded to its call," wrote one such fourteenth-century scholar, Ibn Khaldun. If every instant is too late to avoid ecological catastrophe, then perhaps melancholy is quite as appropriate for us as it was for the survivors of the bubonic plague (should we, in fact, survive).

If every instant is too late, does the concept of future—with an imagined grandchild in my sights as the very basis for this extended essay—lose all value? This is what melancholy from killing what's already dead begs us to ask. Perhaps this melancholy is therefore wisdom.

It is evident that some version of future-thinking, in the form of quarterly profits, corporate strategies, urban plans, military blueprints, actuarial tables, and investment portfolios, is the decision-making lattice of mastery, and therefore environmental destruction. This kind of future-thinking convincingly extends awareness (though not necessarily consciousness), not only to enable us to imagine what might be, but to predict it with certainty, and to execute it. In a documentary film I'm writing, *American Experiment*, an historian of the nineteenth century, Bruce Laverty, describes the first world's fair in the United States, in 1876: "It was this celebration of mankind's dominance of his environment through industry." It was a celebration of mastery. But as the ecological crisis renders its mounting punishments, mastery begins to feel like a sad joke in hubris.

Melancholy is an alternative neural pathway for dealing with extreme rupture; it makes us smaller and more passive and, I would argue, more honest. Do we really believe we control our own destinies?

The experience of enslaved people teaches us that the practice of melancholy, in its most profound form, leads to strength. Slave spirituals evoke dreams and visions of a better place. Through them, enslaved people developed subversive political and personal instincts to gain something from their melancholy, which was dignity, and from dignity empathy, and from empathy will, and from will, strength to transform a nation.

The nature of civil life in a nation based on flawed and insufficient rights is that we fight for them, to expand their reach, and we work diligently against powerful forces when they threaten them. This is the history of a nation whose original promise, that all people are created equal and are therefore entitled to equal treatment under law, has never been fully achieved. The U.S., in civil rights parlance and in the practice of civic life, is always the "future perfect." In this sense, melancholy doesn't cancel future-thinking. Rather it conditions human beings to hope.

For this reason, the possibility of future isn't so easily abandoned, not by wealthy, nor by poor, or even by the condemned. How could we abandon it, this thing contained within us, as in all living things, a potential life? Part of me already occupies tomorrow. (Anyway, my schedule for the rest of the week is full.) I can't, and shouldn't, escape such awareness, a hedge against the miseries of the present. The future that emits from melancholy is prayer, in other words. Perhaps our need for it grows in the face of dark horror.

How to make use of this future, then, a future that demands we not try to master it? If melancholy indeed awakens an honesty of the heart, then we might use it as a doorway to another mode of being, equally honest, but more active and demanding—and therefore more satisfying. That is grief. Melancholy leads us to experience a grief for what has already been lost, the loss that is coming, and for the kind of future we had always been certain would come. Grieving for these things that are fundamentally part of our selves, in an instant we develop a language of shared awareness, a basis for confronting the rapid, shattering changes underway.

Grief forces us to experience a deliberate and pointed focus, on hurt. It insists we submit to the pain of loss; for the things lost become in that moment more present, more real perhaps than they ever had been. This saturated realness is startling in its power to distill, to value, and to judge. This is awakening. As melancholy is a doorway to grief, awakening has the capacity to draw us into a garden of transformation, and that is consciousness.

CONSCIOUSNESS

Not long ago I visited a sixth-grade class in a public school. With the help of a nonprofit organization that encourages young people to learn about social issues and solve community problems, the students had voted to study and try to address plastic pollution in oceans. They were particularly concerned with single-use plastic and had asked me to talk about the failure of recycling, which I had lamented in a newspaper op-ed. With the closing of the Chinese market to American and European recyclable material, Philadelphia officials had decided to temporarily divert half the paper, glass, metal, and plastic the city collected to a trash-to-steam incinerator. This meant that many of us were only pretending to recycle. Given very low rates of recycling historically, this has been the case for forty years.

The students fully understood the dimensions of the problem, that per square mile of ocean there are some 46,000 pieces of plastic; that each American uses 220 pounds of plastic each year; that each year across the globe people use 500 billion plastic bags. With their teacher's guidance they'd come to understand that the oil and chemical companies, packaging manufacturers, and retailers that profit from the overwhelming scale of plastic use have in the U.S. almost extralegal power to influence law and public policy. The students clearly didn't need more information from me; nor were my opinions on the issue any more developed than theirs. But they begged to understand why adults had abandoned their future for convenience today. "Since we are kids, why don't average adults care about this issue?" they asked explicitly. For most of the parents of the children in the room, the teacher told me, the deluge of single-use plastic had barely registered as a problem. For most humans it isn't one.

I'm sure in that instant I attempted a joke. Seeking their allegiance, it was probably at the expense of their parents. I recall my gaze moving from one child's face to another's—seemingly, at least, there was not a Mike among them. Sixth graders can appear to be eight or twenty. So great was the range in height, build, physical maturity that the classroom could have been mistaken for an old-time one-room-schoolhouse. Most of them were actually twelve years old, between the age of my kids and that of my future grandchild. But that future person might as well have been in the room, gazing up from the desk, seeing right through me.

In such a moment my instinct is to write on the board, which I do with the messiest of hands (it can't be helped). Always, my scribbling elicits smirks, especially as I inevitably run out of space or spell something wrong. Finally, writing a bit, I got a little laughter. In large letters, a barrage of lower-case and caps, I roughed out a formula. You didn't think this was math class, did you? I said.

Consciousness = Awareness × Thinking

How does a formula work? I supposed it best to start on the right side. You have to start there to figure an answer. They had asked a question and they needed an answer. Name some things you're aware of, I said. In the middle of the room an arm lifted. "Breathing." Are you always aware of it? No, sometimes I forget. What else? My body. My arms and legs. The window. The posters on the wall. The pencil in his hand. Everything! Really? Are you sure? How about merely everyone in the class? Even that might be impossible.

In a few minutes when school lets out, I asked, how many of you will go to the corner store for a soda or a snack? A plurality of hands went up. And the cashier will put your items in a plastic bag—one of those 500 billion—and hand it to you. Will you be aware of it? The problem is, we aren't aware, someone said. I am! said another student. But if we were to be aware, how would we become so? By what means? On the board, I scrawled:

> Touch
> Taste
> Sight
> Sound
> Smell

And a sixth sense aids our awareness, I said. Let's call it experience. So, the answer is we're always aware of the plastic bag, even when we don't realize it, as long as our senses are functioning properly. Yet clearly, if your parents are any indicators, awareness isn't enough. Perhaps this is why at times we can lose sight of each other, right here in the same room. To "lose sight" doesn't mean to go blind, after all, but to ignore what the eyes are seeing. If we don't want to lose sight, I said, we must think, search for truth and search for meaning both.

In this way we began to consider the other term on the right side of the equation, thinking. Through our animal nature, cognition can multiply awareness, and the result then (on the left side of the equation) is dynamic consciousness, at once cerebral, instinctual, and moral. Consciousness empowers us to see beyond seeing, to adapt, change our minds, confront fear, channel aggression, and reorganize. Drawing on sensory perception and experience, consciousness creates a pathway toward the hyperobject, as if to ground it in the real, the precise, the measurable—in the same way that priests and poets attempt to understand the unknowable God.

The school where I'd come to talk is regarded as one of the city's best. The students are famously (and infamously) bookish, precocious, and intensely prepared. When I asked the class to identify the components of thinking, it took little time to develop this list:

Assertion
Conceptualization
Research
Data collection

Evaluation
Reflection
Contextualization
Interrogation
Choice

Now, armed with cognition, I asked the students to return to the corner store, senses fully multiplied by the mind. But first, an additional question: How long will the average plastic shopping bag remain in use before it's thrown away? Thrown away? Awakening now, the conscious being hears something that no longer makes sense and for a moment forgets about the original question. The conscious being answers, There's only one Earth. Therefore, there's no "away." How long then until the plastic bag is put into a trash bin and then dumped somewhere else on Earth? The plastic bag (made from petroleum extracted through elaborate mechanisms at great cost), which will end up decomposing into invisible microplastic particles on land, in a river, or in the sea—in other words, on Earth—completes its tenure of service in under a quarter hour. Twelve minutes on average,[21] to be precise. With this understanding, in an instant the crinkling plastic bag the store clerk mindlessly fills (likely with other short-lived plastic containers) feels in the hand like a frightening contagion.

21. According to the website The World Counts (https://www.theworldcounts.com/challenges/planet-earth/waste/plastic-bags-used-per-year).

In this way awakening toward consciousness might become a kind of burden. Too much to bear for one single, woke human who can't herself take on the responsibility for the future. I couldn't say to the room full of particularly astute and motivated twelve-year-olds that the burden of consciousness could easily become a tether of despair (and I didn't have time to explain the usefulness of melancholy). I wasn't asked to discuss paralysis. Their lively eyes and quick answers told me that paralysis was exactly what they could not abide.

This refusal, I recognized at once, was the seed of hope. "The cold will relent," wrote Primo Levi of the coming Auschwitz spring, "and we will have one enemy less." In the warm, sunny classroom on what was, by coincidence, winter's final day, the idea of despair seemed as foreign as the plastic bag in conscious hand, and thoroughly untenable.

I hadn't gone into the classroom to collar the students with consciousness. Rather it was the equation itself, the act of multiplying seeing by analyzing, feeling by scrutinizing, hearing by choosing, that I began to realize could lead them, and perhaps all of us, from eco-paralysis. The goal wasn't therefore for them to be "woke," a static end-state. Instead, it is for all of us to awaken continuously. The long path to social change suggests the imperative of the journey and the power of the equation.

I take both solace and inspiration from earlier social movements that began with shifts in consciousness and evolved exponentially. Modern feminism began its first wave perhaps in the eighteenth century with Mary Wollstonecraft or in the nineteenth century with the Black and white female abolitionists who gave themselves political power by boycotting, lecturing, publishing, and petitioning for justice. The awakening, a *causa sui*, led to suffragism, then to workplace and institutional breakthroughs (first female PhDs, law students, etc.), then to tangible shifts in cultural and sexual mores.

With each step, multiplying awareness by thinking produced new modes of protest, law, and behavior, and revised consciousness always sets a new baseline. It's like being granted a new kind of vision.[22] With each use of the equation the baseline value of consciousness widens. This is how, as one instance, the notion of true gender equality evolves exponentially.

And this is why it's possible to assert there's no such thing as throwing something away—because consciousness allows us to question automatic habits. Or to wonder, as a child, why adults don't seem to care if the planet can support the life of future generations—because consciousness demands we question authority. Or to imagine that plants and non-

22. The old kind of vision, for example, would never have seen a need for intersectionality. A consciousness term, intersectionality reveals the hidden connections among racism, poverty, economic inequality, the gender pay gap, and legal inequity, just as #metoo makes the often invisible (and therefore countenanced) sexual assault and harassment against women visible and therefore no longer admissible.

human animals have the kinds of rights we grant to ourselves—because consciousness begs us to ask "what if?" From paralysis to consciousness, the equation confers to us a kind of moral rocket to fit our situation, or at least an existential launch pad.

I find it fitting that Donna J. Haraway's title at the University of California, Santa Cruz, is Distinguished Professor Emerita in the History of Consciousness. I return to Haraway now to employ consciousness—that moral rocket—to help me think and, ultimately, to act. In *Staying with the Trouble*, she scrutinizes the term "Anthropocene" (as well as the more pointed "Capitalocene"). As "Anthropocene" signifies awareness of humanity's impact on Earth, in Haraway's conception "sympoiesis," or becoming with, signifies the complex, interconnected nature of living organisms. Consciousness makes "Anthropocene" feel shallow and oversimplified and leads her to the more richly complicated, revelatory term for the age to come, "Chthulucene" (in Greek mythology *chthonian* gods are gods of the earth and the seas, in specific juxtaposition to heavenly gods).[23] Chthonic beings, she wrote, citing research on sympoiesis, "are a buzzing, stinging, sucking swarm." Despite ourselves, humans are enmeshed in the swarm, which we don't control. In fact, the main rule of the swarm in the Chthulucene is that "we

23. Haraway says that "Chthulucene" is the compound of two Greek roots, *khthôn* and *kainos*, "that together name a kind of timeplace for learning to stay with the trouble of living and dying in response-ability on a damaged earth."

are at stake to each other." In order to benefit ourselves we have to give life to others.

This new consciousness produces new possibilities. "The order is reknitted," Haraway fathoms, anticipating what might happen if our consciousness adjusts to master our own need for mastery. Sympoiesis teaches us "the biotic and abiotic powers of this earth are the main story," not the human over and above all.

In fact, other kinds of creatures are more important to Earth's life systems. If we allow ourselves to accept this reality, then those other beings may deserve to be thought of not as natural resources to be bought and sold—or worse, as threats to be exterminated—but as beings to live alongside, to cultivate, and to love. And if we can achieve such a breakthrough for our fellow plant and animal earthlings, we can do it for ourselves, achieving a primal recognition, a forceful rejection of the circumstances that, like the endless Penthesilean highway, actively and persistently dehumanize: I too am not a commodity. I am neither a demographic nor a market to exploit. I am neither a potential customer nor a source of unending profit. I am neither a data point nor a job, neither valuable skillset nor obsolete functionary. Neither exploiter nor exploitable. Now, for a human being among the many beings, metabolizing oxygen, there is no such thing as paralysis.

Free to act, but what to do? Some readers may wish to see here a menu of steps they can take to save the earth. But such a list doesn't really exist. It's not that things can't be done—of course, we must radically alter our political and economic systems worldwide. The earth can't survive, in any way we would want it to, with the perpetuation of fossil-fuel-based capitalism. It can't survive intensive consumer culture. It can't survive a neoliberal regulatory structure or neo-colonialism. Just how we collectively undo these powerful dynamics is, however, beyond the scope of this work, as the reader surely recognizes by now.

My concern then isn't what to do, but how to approach the doing. My concern is to stimulate ways of thinking about how an individual might reconceive of human life and human society on Earth. And thus, I want to take a moment to consider modes of action. Consciousness reveals, in my interpretation, four of them.

First, grieve, for what's being lost at a disturbing pace—the landscapes, mammals, sea creatures, bugs, trees, forests, ways of life, tastes, smells, cuisines, words, languages, the plenty, the calm of seasons. Grief forces the mind to fixate on what was, to listen for it still ringing in the ears, to taste it on the tongue, to smell it on the breath, to find it in our dreams. Grieve for what is lost already and what will be lost, for what is and what will be missing. Make those things present even as they are slipping away. Grieve prospectively for a grandchild's loss of freedom. When we grieve, we hold on until the loss burns free in our consciousness and we become convinced of the ephemerality of all things. We open ourselves to change, to possibility, and to hope that, in this vast severance of life forms from each other and from the elements that sustain them, new life will emerge. Grief can make us present with this process and open to the heartbreak that will result. For we have to prepare to have our hearts broken, and cruelly so, by our own hands, our own manner of living.

Second, quite related to the first, embrace change, what has already happened and what might come. The British ecologist Chris Thomas is right to scold the environmental movement as reactionary in this sense, insisting on a return to a pure, pastoral past. History suggests strongly that there is no purity, and there never will be. Yet the return to purity is powerfully evocative, especially as it is the goal of so many religious traditions. Fixate then, with all the power of a Sunday sermon, on the fact of change, its peril and possibility. Don't turn away from the horror. In that horror lies the potential for personal, societal, economic, and cultural transformations that may result from the crisis itself and from technological, economic, and political responses and reactions. I would go further to say it is change that we desperately and fundamentally need, to avoid the worst and to ensure the possibility for justice.

As I write this, I'm sitting outside on the bench in front of my row house. It is February, traditionally the coldest month of the year. This may be the warmest February on record. I'm wearing socks, a light shirt, sunglasses. Pear tree blossoms ache to open. Red maple leaves, too. The sidewalk animates with human beings and they are joyful. Elderly couples, college students, children with funny questions. From time to time someone I know stops and in silent accord we acknowledge the balmy weather. Then, nervously: "Beautiful." "Disturbing." "Disturbingly beautiful." More laughter. It's a hedge against discomfort. But the laughter is false. It gets in the way of honesty. Next person who comes along, I tell myself, don't laugh: Accept the change that's happening and just be disturbed; it may come to feel like a strange awakening.

Now, after affirming change, the third mode of action requires accepting that the personal is political and the political personal; there is no difference. Through the personal, we can perform political acts of love for the earth (and for our place in it). Yet various forces in our societies want to simplify the urge to perform, and this limits and weakens the potential of love. Some beg you to change your personal habits, as consumers particularly: eat less meat, stop using plastic water bottles, shop at a farmer's market, recycle, ride public transit, take short showers, stop using straws. Others, who affirm only the value of political solutions, condemn these little hacks as self-indulgent acts of self-absolution that make people feel good while achieving little. They say that only political organizing, mass protests, and structural changes, like shielding political processes from corporate interests or destroying capitalism, will end the ecological crisis. Still others say that, at this point, the only possible solution is to invest in technologies that will quickly remove carbon dioxide from the atmosphere. I will say emphatically that all these things are needed, and furthermore, for moral well-being, they can't be omitted. So, go ahead and eat that way, protest that way, dream that way. All are ways of ritually performing love of Earth. That love must become the goal of our social, political, and economic communities. So, stop flying, if you choose. Stop driving or consuming plastic. Unless these peccadilloes become ends in themselves, they give moral beings ways of acting ethically when all else seems too much to bear. The object of these intentional practices is to transform the paralyzed, complicit human psyche and to align it with political and technological modes to signify an end to paralysis.

Fourth, use the body. This is the potential of the youth climate strike movement: the body can be deployed, alongside other bodies, in spontaneous and planned acts of physical democracy, which at their most successful can topple governments, can launch revolutions. Such acts can extend well beyond protest. The body is a local and localizing concept; it is anchored in time and space, and perhaps, place, and not in the abstract. Feed its hunger for air and earthen matter. Give the body dirt, which is mostly free. Swim in lakes and rivers and oceans, plant gardens, climb mountains, build forests that become invitations to other creatures. One can do so on a tiny city lot or on an abandoned farm or along a river's edge. The supposed gulf between those who believe that carbon dioxide can be reduced significantly through reforestation and those who argue that planting trees is another capitalist diversion from the real crisis (and an ineffectual one at that) is another fictitious division. I bring up forests and trees because we humans relate to them through the essential form of the body. It is a matter of giving life and sustaining the breath we depend on; this is the opposite of taking it away.

SPRING

Awakening now, morning on the damaged earth, and in the northern hemisphere it is, officially, spring. The first cars of the day passing the house, the sun soft against the pastel houses across the street, sage, butter, and sand. Wasn't it only yesterday I was sweeping the merlot leaves of the neighbor's pear tree, which fell in dramatic gusts for a full autumnal month? Now the same tree, stretching across the macadam practically halfway to the other side, prays in stanzas of five and six and seven blossoms, five cloud petals each, expressing a sweet desire for a gentle world. And yet the tree is trapped in its tiny pit and, though pruned by its careful owner, is weak against the winds of spring. It isn't the right kind of tree, after all.

A woman takes her dog for the morning walk; at the corner, the barista sets out the tables and chairs; invisible birdsongs like sound constellations define the sky: here, over there, and further. Is it warm enough to open the window? I'll hear the symphonic beats, up and down, all the better. Stroller wheels and a mother's voice. An infant's despairing cry of hunger. "Caution, bus is turning," says the recorded voice in the distance. A firm yet friendly voice. Several more vehicles enter the roadway, like fishing lines cast into the black stream, following the crank of the gate that lets out the neighbors' cars, the ones with the pastel-painted houses. A horn sounds, as if the pronouncement of cars and more cars is needed.

Spring on damaged earth is the anguish of Penthesilea, what Calvino goes on to name "the inferno of the living," the most fundamental source of our paralysis in the face of ecological crisis.

In his journey through cities of metaphor, Calvino takes the reader from Penthesilea to Theodora. Having faced down invasions of condors, serpents, spiders, woodworms, and termites—each epidemic of one species rising from the natural imbalance caused by the elimination of another—now Theodoran city officials have to confront a horde of poison-resistant rats loose in the city's sewers (the plague indeed taught humans to be wary of rats). After some effort, they are successful. "At last," wrote Calvino with blanched wit, and no lack of melancholy,

> with an extreme massacre, the murderous, versatile ingenuity of mankind defeated the overweening life-force of the enemy.

Perhaps Theodora was the first city of the imagined Anthropocene: Calvino called it the "great cemetery of the animal kingdom." And more so: he declared it "aseptic," clear of germs and fleas.

The triumph of the Theodorans, and by extrapolation the oil barons, is Calvino's—and Haraway's—most terrifying nightmare. It is also, undoubtedly, mine—and ours. This is the inferno "we form by being together," mastering Earth but never ourselves. For isn't that exactly what we must do? Consciousness tells us to envision moving our bodies outside the oil trap toward a way to escape. Haraway imagines the possibility of freedom from the demands of dominance. "The world is not finished," she wrote hopefully of a new world to come. In this possible future, "biotic and abiotic powers of this earth are the main story," not only, or primarily, human beings.

Much after the elimination of the rats in Calvino's Theodora, the fauna of history, preserved only in the city's archives and libraries, all of a sudden begin to awaken. "Leaping from the capitals and drainpipes, perching at the sleepers' bedside," the vanquished fauna haunt their troubled human conquerors, who are—as we ourselves are presently learning to experience—perhaps tortured by the guilt and grief of loss. In this interpretation of what transpires in Theodora, the haunting is therefore a deserved, infernal punishment for destroying all that made us and sustained our humanity. Does Calvino mean us to see what we will have done unless we pull back now? Extinction and ecosystem unraveling will define our age of loss (that so far, self-tricking, we believe to be an age of plenty). Soon, the signs of dead and defeated Earth will be every-where, and impossible to ignore. We won't be able to hide the Great Barrier Reef, now substantially weak-ened from bouts of bleaching, in an archival museum. Nor the ruins of Almir Suruí's Amazon home.

But perhaps Calvino meant the revival of stricken fauna literally. Human beings can go to sleep at night believing they've smothered Earth, but the immensity and intricacy of Earth life can't be entirely choked off. Spring will come, somehow, in some form, no mat-ter. The question for us, as humans, is its quality. Our decision to make is thus between degrees of domi-nance and degrees of deference. The immediate end to fossil fuel use, mining, and the damming of rivers would constitute extreme and radical deference.

Concluding *Invisible Cities*, Calvino suggested that deference won't be easy, for we've grown so accus-tomed to dominance's inferno. Mastering ourselves and our perceived needs to make adequate and ample room for other beings will require, according to him, "constant vigilance and apprehension." For years I've kept his urging on the wall facing my desk:

Seek and learn to recognize who and what, in the midst of the inferno, are not inferno, then make them endure, give them space.[24]

24. Many observers of the COVID-19 pandemic have noted that while human beings retreated, en masse, into quarantine, under stay-at-home orders, not only did pollution drop but the sudden absence of people created an opening for other beings to share space, to make themselves at home.

I've read this passage a thousand times. I've recited it in front of audiences. It's the twentieth century's prayer for the twenty-first.

Late in the afternoon, my window remains open. What is not inferno? The birds haven't ever paused. Are they somehow more sonorous now, late in the day? For a moment the cars relent. Their absence feels like an opening to the future. Consciousness = Awareness × Thinking. Make the swarm endure. Give it space. Give it life. The wind zings and puffs the leaves of the slender urban forest, April's ecstatic green of birch and hemlock and maple rising above the pastel row houses, innocent again. A block away, or two, or three, I hear a wind chime shimmering and resting, rising and calming, the wind setting pace, the chime like a tiny sound cathedral to capture the spirit, to translate it into rhythm, into song. Listen to it playing, carefree.

Philadelphia, September 2018–June 2020

acknowledgments

This work is a testament to community. We think together and writing is an act of thinking. In that spirit I have so many to acknowledge for thinking along with me. First, Rona Buchalter and Lena Popkin, who both read the manuscript in its earliest forms, and Isaak Popkin for designing the cover: I owe you much more than gratitude for thinking with me day after day. My deepest thanks also to Andrew Ferrett, Jeffrey McMahon, Kate Oxx, Peter Siskind, Anders Uhl, and Peter Woodall for forcing me to think a little harder about the human relationship to the natural world, with more precision, with fewer assumptions. To Xandra van der Eijk for hours of thinking together at the Valley of the Possible in southern Chile (where the cover photograph was taken), and to Mirla Klijn and Olaf Boswijk for bringing me there, along with Darko Lagunas, Mark IJzerman, Juan Ferrer, and Sébastien Robert, to sharpen our senses, and our thinking, amidst ecological crisis. To Bethany Wiggin, director of the Penn Program in Environmental Humanities, for engaging with the work in manuscript form and helping me present it at the Rosenbach Museum and Library. To Scott Knowles, of Drexel University, for allowing me to present a draft at the Academy of Natural Sciences. To the book's editor, Ann de Forest, for her firm and loving guidance and for drawing out, like an alchemist, the most promising ideas. To Ann and publisher Doug Gordon and the other members of the Working Writers Group: Miriam Seidel, Vikram Paralkar, Mark Lyons, Louis Greenstein, Debra Leigh Scott, and David Sanders. This book doesn't exist without you.